More Praise for . . .
The Performance Appraisal Question and Answer Book:

"An enlightening, practical, and valuable tool. Dick has taken the sometime confusing and frightening problem of performance appraisal and provided effective approaches and answers that can be adapted to any organization. It is a MUST for the human resources professional's library."

—William K. Hill
Human Resources Director
City of Winston-Salem (NC)

"Dick Grote clearly and eloquently presents a very practical guide for navigating the often-murky waters of the performance appraisal process. *The Performance Appraisal Question and Answer Book* is a must-read for all who are captivated with the notion that the development, administration, and oversight of an effective performance management system is not only possible, but indispensable to the organizational life of any business."

—Michael S. Sorrells
Deputy Commissioner for Human Resources
Georgia Department of Juvenile Justice

"Much has been written and debated about the value of performance management systems. However, the fact remains that top-performing companies have rigorous performance management systems. *The Performance Appraisal Question and Answer Book* is a must-have handbook for every manager's most complex issue: performance."

—Don Langewisch
Performance Systems Manager
ChevronTexaco Corporation

The
PERFORMANCE APPRAISAL
QUESTION and ANSWER BOOK

A SURVIVAL GUIDE
FOR MANAGERS

Dick Grote

AMACOM
American Management Association
New York • Atlanta • Brussels • Buenos Aires • Chicago • London • Mexico City
San Francisco • Shanghai • Tokyo • Toronto • Washington, D.C.

Special discounts on bulk quantities of AMACOM books are available to corporations, professional associations, and other organizations. For details, contact Special Sales Department, AMACOM, a division of American Management Association, 1601 Broadway, New York, NY 10019.
Tel.: 212-903-8316. Fax: 212-903-8083.
Web site: www.amacombooks.org

This publication is designed to provide accurate and authoritative information in regard to the subject matter covered. It is sold with the understanding that the publisher is not engaged in rendering legal, accounting, or other professional service. If legal advice or other expert assistance is required, the services of a competent professional person should be sought.

Library of Congress Cataloging-in-Publication Data

Grote, Richard C.
    The performance appraisal question and answer book: survival guide for managers / Dick Grote.
        p.   cm.
    Includes index.
    ISBN 0-8144-0747-1 (hardcover)
    ISBN 0-8144-7151-X (paperback)
    1. Employees—Rating of.   2. Performance standards.   I. Title.
HF5549.5 .R3   G642   2002
658.3'125—dc21

                                                          2002002171

Printing number

10 9 8 7 6 5 4 3 2 1

Contents

Introduction

In sophisticated, well-managed organizations, performance appraisal is the single most important management tool. No other management process has as much influence over individuals' careers and work lives. Used well, performance appraisal is the most powerful instrument that organizations have to mobilize the energy of every employee of the enterprise toward the achievement of strategic goals. Used well, performance appraisal can focus every person's attention on the company's mission, vision, and values. But used poorly, the procedure quickly becomes the butt of jokes and the target of Dilbert lampoons.

For over thirty years, I have helped organizations create highly effective, world-class performance appraisal systems. In this time, I have learned what actually qualifies as "best practice." I have learned how to help companies incorporate the most effective procedures there are for guiding, directing, assessing, and developing human performance. I have helped them use performance appraisal to achieve important organizational objectives. I have taught their managers how to become masters of this challenging and difficult management technique.

Make no mistake. Performance appraisal is difficult. Doing performance appraisal is like being in the Olympics of management. Few people ever get the chance to participate; even fewer are true masters. My goal in this book is to make you and your organization a true master of performance appraisal.

The questions in this book have come from two sources. First, they have come from the thousands of questions I have responded to from top executives, human resources professionals, managers, and individuals both in my consulting practice in helping companies create a new appraisal system, and in the management seminars I have conducted to help managers maximize the effectiveness of their existing systems.

Second, questions poured forth from hundreds of managers in response to the e-mail I sent clients, colleagues, and friends just before I began writing this book. I explained the project that I had undertaken and asked them to send me the most difficult and important questions they had about performance appraisal. They responded almost overwhelmingly. The questions in this book are real; they represent the actual issues of managers whose goal is to create a climate of performance excellence.

The book begins with an overview of why performance appraisal is an incredibly powerful but underappreciated management technique. Chapters 2 through 5 deal with the four phases of an effective performance management system: performance planning, execution, assessment, and review.

The sixth chapter deals specifically with the performance appraisal form. Yes, there is an ideal form. In Chapter 6, I will tell you exactly what an ideal appraisal form looks like—what it contains and how to create one.

But we all know that performance appraisal isn't a form. It's a system. In Chapter 7, I will explain exactly how the most effective performance appraisal process works.

Chapter 8 deals with building performance excellence. In this chapter I will cover two critical issues: First, I will describe what actually works in developing human talent. Second, I will tell you how to solve people problems when they arise.

The last chapter is the shortest. In this final chapter, I will respond to only one question. But this question is the most important of all the questions, and the one that truly does deserve a chapter all to itself: Now that all is said and done, is performance appraisal really all that important? Yes, it is, and I'll tell you why.

For almost thirty years, I have been a consultant whose work focuses exclusively on performance management. My goal is to help organizations create performance management systems that reward excellence and demand personal responsibility; to help their managers understand how to maximize the contributions of every person on their team. I know that the single most important competency required to build performance excellence is not knowledge or skill or desire: It is courage. I hope this book gives every reader the incentive to muster the courage to build performance excellence into every aspect of life.

This book will probably generate as many questions as it answers. If you have a question—or an insight, or a success story—please share them with me at DickGrote@GroteConsulting.com or visit my website, www.PerformanceAppraisal.com.

The
PERFORMANCE
APPRAISAL
QUESTION and
ANSWER BOOK

Chapter 1

The Importance of Performance Appraisal

1.1 What is "performance appraisal"?

Performance appraisal is a formal management system that provides for the evaluation of the quality of an individual's performance in an organization. The appraisal is usually prepared by the employee's immediate supervisor. The procedure typically requires the supervisor to fill out a standardized assessment form that evaluates the individual on several different dimensions and then discusses the results of the evaluation with the employee.

Tell Me More

Too often, performance appraisal is seen merely as a once-a-year drill mandated by the personnel department. But in organizations that take performance appraisal seriously and use the system well, it is used as an ongoing process and not merely as an annual event. In these companies, performance appraisal follows a four-phase model:

Phase 1: Performance Planning. At the beginning of the year, the manager and individual get together for a performance-planning meeting. In this hour-long session they discuss what the person will achieve over the next twelve months (the key responsibilities of the person's job and the goals and projects the person will work on) and how the person will do the job (the behaviors and competencies the organization expects of its members). They typically also discuss the individual's development plans.

Phase 2: Performance Execution. Over the course of the year the employee works to achieve the goals, objectives, and key responsibilities of the job. The manager provides coaching and feedback to the individ-

1

ual to increase the probability of success. He creates the conditions that motivate and resolves any performance problems that arise. Midway through the year—perhaps even more frequently—they meet to review the individual's performance thus far against the plans and goals that they discussed in the performance-planning meeting.

Phase 3: Performance Assessment. As the time for the formal performance appraisal nears, the manager reflects on how well the subordinate has performed over the course of the year, assembles the various forms and paperwork that the organization provides to make this assessment, and fills them out. The manager may also recommend a change in the individual's compensation based on the quality of the individual's work. The completed assessment form is usually reviewed and approved by the appraiser's boss. Others—perhaps the department head or the compensation manager—may also review and approve the assessment.

Phase 4: Performance Review. The manager and the subordinate meet, usually for about an hour. They review the appraisal form that the manager has written and talk about how well the person performed over the past twelve months. At the end of the review meeting they set a date to meet again to hold a performance-planning discussion for the next twelve months, at which point the performance management process starts anew.

Of course there may be many individual variations on the basic theme, but most sophisticated companies generally follow this four-phase process. Figure 1-1 illustrates the basic four-phase process.

1.2   Where did performance appraisals come from?

There are early references to performance appraisal in America going back over a hundred years. The federal Civil Service Commission's merit rating system was in place in 1887. Lord & Taylor introduced performance appraisal in 1914. Many companies were influenced by Frederick Taylor's "scientific management" efforts of the early twentieth century and concocted performance appraisals.

Before World War II, however, very few organizations conducted any formal performance appraisals. A handful of companies and the military were the only ones using the procedure regularly. Most appraisals that were done concentrated more on an individual's personality and traits than on actual achievements against goals and formal analyses of the behaviors that produced those results.

Figure 1-1. Strategy-based performance management.

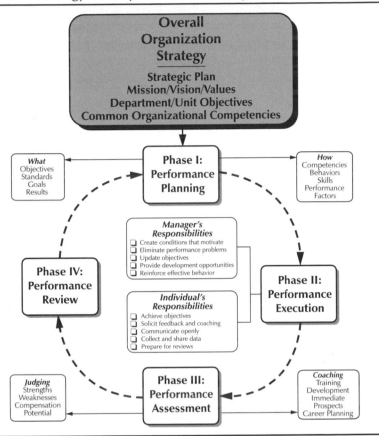

Source: Grote Consulting Corporation.

Then, in the 1950s Peter Drucker's novel idea of management by objectives (MBO) and Douglas McGregor's book *The Human Side of Enterprise,* which introduced his notions of Theory X and Theory Y, gained a lot of attention. A few companies moved from a mere trait assessment to the development of a procedure that concentrated on goal setting and made the appraisal process a shared responsibility between the individual and the manager. From the work of Drucker and McGregor, the performance appraisal procedure has grown to the point where a huge majority of companies now have a formal appraisal system.

Tell Me More

"Effective development of managers," McGregor wrote in a 1957 *Harvard Business Review* article, "does not include coercing them (no matter how benevolently) into acceptance of the goals of the enterprise, nor does it mean manipulating their behavior to suit organizational needs. Rather, it calls for creating a relationship within which a man can take responsibility for developing his own potentialities, plan for himself, and learn from putting his plans into action."

Drucker's initial proposal of an MBO process to replace trait appraisals and McGregor's integration of a "Theory Y" approach into the appraisal process produced a change in the way organizations went about assessing the contributions of their members. General Electric was singled out by McGregor as an example of a company that was using an MBO/Theory Y approach to performance appraisal. GE conducted a truly scientific study in the early 1960s to test the effectiveness of its annual, comprehensive appraisal approach. It found that:

- Criticism has a negative effect on achievement of goals.
- Praise has little effect one way of the other.
- Performance improves most when specific goals are established.
- Defensiveness resulting from critical appraisal produces inferior performance.
- Coaching should be a day-to-day, not a once-a-year activity.
- Mutual goal setting, not criticism, improves performance.
- Interviews designed primarily to improve a man's performance should not at the same time weigh his salary or promotion in the balance.
- Participation by the employee in the goal-setting procedure helps produce favorable results.

These findings remain today as valid as they were when GE first developed them.

Performance appraisal as a management tool spread quickly in the 1950s, when about half of 400 employers surveyed reported using appraisal systems. Today, depending on the survey, somewhere between three-quarters and nine-tenths of all companies use a formal performance appraisal procedure.

1.3   What is the purpose of performance appraisal?

Performance appraisal serves over a dozen different organizational purposes:

- Providing feedback to employees about their performance
- Determining who gets promoted
- Facilitating layoff or downsizing decisions
- Encouraging performance improvement
- Motivating superior performance
- Setting and measuring goals
- Counseling poor performers
- Determining compensation changes
- Encouraging coaching and mentoring
- Supporting manpower planning or succession planning
- Determining individual training and development needs
- Determining organizational training and development needs
- Confirming that good hiring decisions are being made
- Providing legal defensibility for personnel decisions
- Improving overall organizational performance

Tell Me More

Providing Feedback. Providing feedback is the most common justification for an organization to have a performance appraisal system. Through its performance appraisal process the individual learns exactly how well she did during the previous twelve months and can then use that information to improve her performance in the future. In this regard, performance appraisal serves another important purpose by making sure that the boss's expectations are clearly communicated.

Facilitating Promotion Decisions. Almost everyone in an organization wants to get ahead. How should the company decide who gets the brass rings? Performance appraisal makes it easier for the organization to make good decisions about making sure that the most important positions are filled by the most capable individuals.

Facilitating Layoff or Downsizing Decisions. If promotions are what everybody wants, layoffs are what everybody wishes to avoid. But when economic realities force an organization to downsize, performance appraisal helps make sure that the most talented individuals are retained and that only the organization's marginal performers are cut loose.

Encouraging Performance Improvement. How can anyone improve if he doesn't know how he's doing right now? A good performance appraisal points out areas where individuals need to improve their performance.

Motivating Superior Performance. This is another classic reason for having a performance appraisal system. Performance appraisal helps motivate people to deliver superior performance in several ways. First, the appraisal process helps them learn just what it is that the organization considers to be "superior." Second, since most people want to be seen as superior performers, a performance appraisal process provides them with a means to demonstrate that they actually are. Finally, performance appraisal encourages employees to avoid being stigmatized as inferior performers (or, often worse, as merely "average").

Setting and Measuring Goals. Goal setting has consistently been demonstrated as a management process that generates superior performance. The performance appraisal process is commonly used to make sure that every member of the organization sets and achieves effective goals.

Counseling Poor Performers. Not everyone meets the organization's standards. Performance appraisal forces managers to confront those whose performance is not meeting the company's expectations.

Determining Compensation Changes. This is another classic use of performance appraisal. Almost every organization believes in pay for performance. But how can pay decisions be made if there is no measure of performance? Performance appraisal provides the mechanism to make sure that those who do better work receive more pay.

Encouraging Coaching and Mentoring. Managers are expected to be good coaches to their team members and mentors to their protégés. Performance appraisal identifies the areas where coaching is necessary and encourages managers to take an active coaching role.

Supporting Manpower Planning. Well-managed organizations regularly assess their bench strength to make sure that they have the talent in their ranks that they will need for the future. Companies need to determine who and where their most talented members are. They need to identify the departments that are rich with talent and the ones that are suffering a talent drought. Performance appraisal gives companies the tool they need to make sure they have the intellectual horsepower required for the future.

Determining Individual Training and Development Needs. If the performance appraisal procedure includes a requirement that individual development plans be determined and discussed, individuals can then make good decisions about the skills and competencies they need to acquire to make a greater contribution to the company. As a result, they increase their chances of promotion and lower their odds of layoff.

Determining Organizational Training and Development Needs. Would the organization be better off sending all of its managers and professionals through a customer service training program or one on effective decision making? By reviewing the data from performance appraisals, training and development professionals can make good decisions about where the organization should concentrate company-wide training efforts.

Validating Hiring Decisions. Is the company hiring stars, or is it filling itself with trolls? Only when the performance of newly hired individuals is assessed can the company learn whether it is hiring the right people.

Providing Legal Defensibility for Personnel Decisions. Almost any personnel decision—termination, denial of a promotion, transfer to another department—can be subjected to legal scrutiny. If one of these is challenged, the company must be able to demonstrate that the decision it made was not based on the individual's race or handicap or any other protected aspect. A solid record of performance appraisals greatly facilitates legal defensibility when a complaint about discrimination is made.

Improving Overall Organizational Performance. This is the most important reason for an organization to have a performance appraisal system. A performance appraisal procedure allows the organization to communicate performance expectations to every member of the team and assess exactly how well each person is doing. When everyone is clear on the expectations and knows exactly how he is performing against them, this will result in an overall improvement in organizational success.

1.4 The performance management process in our organization has conflicting purposes. We use it to determine merit increases and performance feedback for work done during the previous twelve months, to determine training needs, and as a key tool in succession planning. Can one procedure really serve all those functions well?

One of the fundamental problems with performance management is that we load one system with too many expectations.

It is very difficult for one management system to serve so many objectives well, particularly when there is pressure from managers to reduce the number of meetings required and to streamline the form to a one-page document.

Here's a workable solution. First, communicate the importance of performance appraisal to everyone in the organization. In particular, let everyone know that the process is used as a fundamental determinant of many decisions that affect people in a very personal way. Second, review your appraisal instrument to make sure that it can provide the data the organization and appraisers need to serve all of the different purposes (realize that this may make the appraisal form more complex and comprehensive). Finally, consider using different processes and holding separate meetings to deal with each of the areas that a performance management system addresses.

1.5   How many meetings should I have with an employee to talk about performance?

You should have a minimum of two meetings. You'll hold one at the beginning of the year—the performance planning meeting—where you will talk about the important results to be achieved over the next twelve months. In this meeting you and your subordinate will review the job description, the organization's mission and vision and values statements, your department's goals, and the most important items on the performance appraisal form.

The second mandatory meeting will be at the end of the year, after you have written the appraisal and had it approved by your boss. This is the performance review meeting. You and the individual will discuss the performance appraisal, talk about the individual's achievements over the past twelve months, review his development needs, and then plan for the next twelve months.

Besides these two mandatory meetings, however, good managers meet with their people to talk about performance on a routine and regular basis. They also conduct a formal midterm review halfway through the year.

1.6   All these meetings take too much time. Why should I spend all this time doing performance appraisal when I've got much better things to do?

Does performance appraisal take too long? Let's calculate just how much time the performance management process takes. The planning meeting lasts forty-five minutes to an hour, once a year. Writing some-body's performance appraisal takes another hour, maybe an hour and a half. And the performance appraisal discussion takes about forty-five minutes with most people.

That's about three hours. Add another three hours for preparation, thinking, and planning. Now you're up to six hours per person.

There are exactly 2,000 work hours in a year (8 hours a day $\times$ 5 days a week $\times$ 50 weeks a year = 2,000). Six hours therefore represents 0.3 percent of a manager's time devoted to performance management for each employee. What "better things" do you have to do?

Too often, the complaint about performance management taking too much time results because neither appraisers nor appraisees have a clear picture of exactly what is expected of the process and what the benefits of an effective performance management process are. Obvi-ously, if people don't understand why they are doing something and they don't know how to do it well, it will seem like a timewaster.

1.7 If performance appraisal is truly important, why is it the butt of so many jokes and the target of Dilbert cartoons?

There are several reasons performance appraisal doesn't work as well as it might:

- *No Ownership.* Too often, neither the manager nor the individual has any sense of ownership. They weren't involved in the design or administration of the system. They frequently are not trained to use it effectively. Finally, human resources rarely asks about their reactions to and opinions of the system (and ignores any suggestions they make to improve it).

- *Bad News.* Managers don't like to deliver negative messages to people with whom they must work, and whom they often like on a personal basis. Employees don't like to be told that they are not quite as good as they think they are. Negative messages generate defensive reactions and promote hostility, rather than serve as useful perform-ance feedback.

- *Adverse Impact.* Both managers and employees know that bad reviews adversely impact a person's career. Managers are conscious of the permanence of the paper trail that follows formal appraisal and are often hesitant to commit negative feedback to writing.

- *Scarce Rewards.* The organization usually offers few formal rewards for taking the process seriously and probably no informal rewards. On the other hand, there may be many informal rewards for not delivering unpopular messages.

- *Personal Reflection.* Managers hesitate to give unfavorable appraisals for fear that the appearance of unsatisfactory work by a subordinate will reflect badly on the manager's ability to select and develop subordinates. Lack of candor in evaluation is a way of hiding one's dirty laundry.

- *EEO Terror.* Managers fear that if they give an honest but unsatisfactory appraisal to a black or handicapped employee, they'll be hauled off to court for discrimination.

Although it's easy to poke fun at performance appraisal (and the way performance appraisal is carried out by many managers and many organizations makes it a worthy candidate for Dilbert lampoons), performance appraisal performs a function of enormous value to an organization and to all of its members. Performance appraisal answers the questions that everyone in an organization genuinely asks: Boss, how am I doing? Is my work satisfactory? Do I have a bright future here?

1.8   W. Edwards Deming, the quality guru, said that performance appraisals were an organizational evil that should be abolished. Was he wrong?

Yes. Deming and others in the quality movement correctly noted that individuals are rarely the responsible parties when quality problems arise. More frequently, poor quality is a function of system breakdowns and bad processes, not individual failures. Deming urged organizations to concentrate on system problems and not human problems. That approach may work well for operations management, but it leads to seriously defective people management procedures.

Tell Me More

Deming made a simple observation: All processes and operations are either within tolerance or they are out of tolerance in a positive or negative direction. That same principle is the one under which performance appraisal operates. An individual's performance is either that which the organization expects, or it varies in a positive way and exceeds expectations, or it varies in a negative way and fails to meet expectations. Performance appraisal is simply the application of a central idea of the quality movement to the human dimension.

But there is a flaw in applying quality principles to human performance. Quality experts operate on the basis that if operations are performing properly and according to standard, they should be left alone. Attention should be concentrated only on those aspects that vary from the norm. If this notion is applied to human performance, the great majority of workers in an organization will be ignored by the organization because their performance is not out of whack in either a positive or negative direction.

To ensure high quality of products and processes, it may be important to let alone things that are operating properly and concentrate on the exceptions. In managing human performance that approach is a serious mistake. One of the most frequent complaints people have of their organizations is that they get little attention when they do what is expected. Only when they truly excel (which, for most people, is rare) or completely screw up (which also is rare) do they get any attention from the boss.

Performance appraisal forces managers and organizations to focus on the fact that the great majority of employees are doing exactly what the organization expects of them and that the company recognizes and reinforces their contributions.

1.9 Even if they try to be objective, managers can't help but discriminate on the basis of race, sex, age, and other illegal considerations. Isn't performance appraisal actually a very biased process?

No. While many people believe that managers discriminate, either deliberately or unconsciously, in their appraisal ratings, research on performance appraisal indicates that performance ratings are remarkably bias-free.

Tell Me More

In a major research project published in *Psychological Bulletin*, Frank Landy and James Farr reviewed all of the research that had been conducted over a thirty-year period on performance ratings. They studied every aspect of performance ratings: the effect of different rating formats and the influence of varying rater and ratee characteristics.

What part did age and sex and race and education play? Here's what they found:

Sex. "In the majority of studies, there has been no consistent effect of rater sex on ratings obtained in various contexts." In other words, men are neither tougher nor more lenient than women. Nor do men rate women more gently or strictly than they do other men, or vice versa. Sex appears to be irrelevant.

Race. They were able to find one study in which supervisory raters gave higher ratings to subordinates of their own race than to subordinates of a different race. But that study also indicated that the difference in ratings was only on the order of 2 percent—more important to the statistician or academician than to the line manager or human resources professional. As far as peer ratings, the research shows that race has no effect.

Age. Two different studies explored whether age made any difference. One study found that younger supervisors were less lenient than older ones; the other found no difference at all.

Education. Only one study indicated that the supervisor's education level has any effect on how supervisors rated subordinates. The raters concluded that rater education was of no practical importance.

The Landy and Farr report did repudiate one universally accepted piece of folk wisdom—that peers are tougher on each other than bosses are. Peers are not tougher than bosses, they discovered. Three different studies reported that supervisors were less lenient in their ratings than were the peers of the ratee. Two other studies also found that supervisors were more consistent in their ratings than were peers.

Performance appraisal is not inherently discriminatory. There are several reasons for inaccurate accusations of discrimination. First, consider an organization whose managers have not done a very good job of telling people the truth about their performance over the years. A new manager with tougher standards and a greater willingness to tell people about their shortcomings takes over the work group. Now people who for years have been rated as fully acceptable will be evaluated as unacceptable. Unwilling to accept this new and more realistic evaluation of their contributions, the poor performers will raise the discrimination flag.

Second, people in general have higher opinions of their performance than is warranted. The person who receives a "marginal" rating may interpret a poor review as a function of the appraiser's bias rather than her own poor performance.

Third, some people who are protected by reason of race, sex, or national origin will use that as a shield to avoid working hard and producing results. They figure that they can scare weak managers into giving them an inflated review by threatening legal action if the boss tells the truth about them. Too often, unfortunately, they're correct.

1.10 What are the legal requirements for a performance appraisal system?

First, there is no legal requirement that a company must have a performance appraisal system. No law compels an organization to review the performance of its members, just as no law requires a company to produce annual budgets or provide good customer service. Conducting performance reviews, creating budgets, and giving good service are simply accepted management practices and very good ideas.

If a company does choose to have a performance appraisal system, it must be sure that the system complies with the laws. In the eyes of the law a performance appraisal is an employment test. It is thus scrutinized in a manner similar to that of other aspects of the employment process: initial recruitment, selection and hiring, promotion, compensation, and termination. As a result, the legal requirements for performance appraisal systems are similar to those for other selection tests.

1.11 How do I make sure that our performance appraisal system is legally defensible?

No appraisal system is immune to legal challenge. Nonetheless, the risk of legal difficulties can be minimized if seven basic good management practices are followed.

1. Base the performance appraisal on an analysis of the job.
2. Define your performance dimensions in behavioral terms and support assessments with observable, objective evidence.
3. Keep things simple.

4. Monitor and audit for discrimination.
5. Train raters to assess performance accurately and to conduct effective appraisal discussions.
6. Provide for upper-management review before the appraisal is reviewed with the individual.
7. Provide some appeal mechanism.

Tell Me More

Base the performance appraisal on an analysis of the job. Courts are skeptical of subjective, trait-based rating systems for two reasons: They leave an enormous amount of room for the biases of raters to influence the outcomes, and they are not directly related to specific job responsibilities. Organizations, however, are not required to conduct exhaustive analyses of each job in the company as a condition of doing performance appraisal. A job analysis can be built directly into the appraisal process itself.

When an individual and manager discuss the important goals and objectives that the individual will address during the course of the year and against which his performance will be appraised, that's a job analysis. If a manager evaluates the specific behaviors and expected conduct and demeanor required to perform according to the company's expectations, and then discusses these expectations and their importance with each subordinate, that's a job analysis.

When a supervisor and subordinate together determine what results the subordinate should concentrate on producing over the upcoming year, and they also discuss how the subordinate will go about generating those results—the behaviors and competencies that must be demonstrated—a legitimate job analysis has been conducted.

Define your performance dimensions in behavioral terms and support assessments with observable, objective evidence. Not every job is amenable to results-based, quantitative measurement. For many jobs, success depends on such attributes as cooperation, dependability, customer relations, attitude, and other even more abstract attributes.

Are these attributes important? Of course—no one would argue that they are not critically important. Who would want an employee who is uncooperative, undependable, hostile with customers, and surly toward everyone else? Can they be measured and described? Of course they can. The challenge comes in finding a way to measure and evaluate these critical but intangible attributes.

Completely quantifiable measures of performance do not always exist. If they did, everyone would use them. In fact, if there were complete numerical measures for every aspect of every job, performance appraisal systems themselves would probably not be necessary—the data would speak for themselves. But with most jobs, there are few absolutely direct and impartial measures of an individual's performance, particularly when successful performance is less dependent on performing countable acts than it is on such vital but elusive responsibilities as the ability to recognize and take advantage of opportunities, the ability to build a committed work team, or the ability to recognize obstacles before they become serious interferences.

The answer is to describe the performance in behavioral terms. Write a description of what a master performer in each of these areas would be likely to do. Provide this description to the appraiser and ask the appraiser to assess how often the individual performed in the way described.

By changing the rating scale to eliminate the requirement that raters evaluate the goodness or badness of performance (e.g., unsatisfactory/fair/competent/superior) and replacing it with a scale that reflects how often the individual performs as a true master might (e.g., rarely/sometimes/frequently/always), the organization reduces the possibility of legal challenge and increase the ability of the rater to conduct a more meaningful discussion.

Keep things simple. Complex forms that attempt to provide a total and complete evaluation of every aspect of the individual's performance only frustrate managers and allow their biases to overcome their objectivity. The ideal performance appraisal form (discussed in detail in Chapter 6) asks the appraiser to evaluate the individual in five areas:

1. *Organizational Core Competencies.* These are the skills, attributes, traits, or behaviors that are expected of everyone in the organization, regardless of job or organizational level. "Ethics and integrity" and "customer focus" might be core competencies that everyone in the company will be expected to demonstrate.

2. *Job Family Competencies.* These are the competencies that apply to major job families. "Job family" is a convenient way to think about groupings of individual jobs that share characteristics. Some typical job families are managerial/supervisor, sales, professional/technical, and operations. "Planning and organizing" and "conceptual thinking" might be competencies assessed of everyone whose job is in the professional/technical job family, whereas "safety" may only show up on the form used for employees whose job falls into the operations job family.

3. *Key Job Responsibilities.* These are the major responsibilities or duties of the individual's position. An ideal job description would specify exactly what the key job responsibilities are.

4. *Projects and Goals.* These are the individual's activities that go beyond the specific tasks and duties outlined in a job description.

5. *Major Achievements.* Every performance appraisal form should require the manager to identify a small number of major accomplishments of the individual over the course of the year.

Monitor and audit for discrimination. Two areas need to be monitored to make sure that the organization faces the least amount of risk from legal challenge: first, the company's performance appraisal procedures themselves; second, the personnel decisions that are based on performance appraisal data.

The first area involves determining whether the average appraisal results of members of a protected class are significantly different from the results of the majority. However, if a complete statistical analysis of a large organization were made, it's unlikely that there would be no departments or other organizational units where the average evaluation of one group of employees (e.g., black female employees) was not significantly lower than the average rating given another group of employees (e.g., white males). Does this mean that the company is discriminating against black females in favor of white males? No. These are normal and expected variations. Even if the average appraisal results of a protected class are significantly different from those of the majority, it does not follow that the appraisals are biased or that the appraisal system is automatically illegal.

Hot Tip

If the company's performance appraisal system ends up with the assignment of each individual to a specific rating category (e.g., marginal, fair, competent, superior, and distinguished), an analysis should be made to determine whether there is any significant difference in the ratings given to minority group members versus the ratings of organization members as a whole.

The second area to monitor is the way decisions that are based on performance appraisal are made. In addition to making sure that the performance appraisals themselves are not discriminatory, it is equally important to make sure that personnel decisions that are based on data that the appraisals provide—compensation, promotion, selection for special training programs, termination—are also nondiscriminatory.

Monitoring and auditing cannot solve problems. They can bring troublesome situations to light. Once the organization knows where it stands, corrective action can be taken where the need is greatest.

Train raters to assess performance accurately and to conduct effective appraisal discussions. Ideally, every organization should conduct a formal and comprehensive training program that all managers are required to attend as a precondition for their conducting performance appraisals. They should also conduct annual refresher training for all appraisers just before they begin the annual task of assessing performance and discussing the results.

In the absence of this ideal, virtually every organization can afford to conduct a one-hour briefing session to help raters carry out their responsibility with some minimal degree of confidence. Just providing this minimal level of training alone, in addition to the actual benefits it provides in assuring more accurate appraisals, also is useful in case the organization is charged with discrimination growing out of performance appraisal.

Even if training raters is not possible at all, there is probably no reason why raters cannot be provided with a page or two of instructions covering the most important aspects of the performance evaluation process with some basic suggestions for discussing performance reviews that will reduce the organization's exposure to legal challenge. At a minimum, all appraisers need to be told to:

- Be prepared to provide specific examples to support performance ratings, particularly those where the employee is rated as less than satisfactory.
- Avoid any discussion that refers to a person's membership in a protected group.
- Maintain rapport and a positive atmosphere during the discussion, even when discussing problem areas and the consequences of failure to improve. Many discrimination complaints result not from direct acts of discriminating but from an individual's belief that he was treated unfairly or caught off guard by an unexpectedly low rating that was not fully explained and justified.

Finally, just giving appraisers a few examples of well-completed appraisal forms can increase their ability to do a good job.

Provide for upper-management review before the appraisal is discussed with the individual. Most organizations require the manager who completes the appraisal form to have it reviewed and approved by his boss before it is given to the employee. This is a good idea. Managers who might be capricious or arbitrary (let alone directly discriminatory) in their appraisal assessments may tend to be a tad more cautious knowing that their direct supervisor must review and approve what they have written first.

Upper managers should be encouraged to do more than rubber-stamp the appraisals that are sent up to them for review. Most of the time, senior managers have a reasonably good idea of the overall quality of performance of the people in their department, even though the individuals may be two or three organizational levels down. If the vice president who's reviewing a bunch of performance appraisals simply takes one appraisal and says to the appraiser, "I was surprised to see that you ended up rating Patty as superior (or distinguished or unsatisfactory). Tell me about how you came up with that rating," this question alone will encourage increased diligence in performance assessment in the future.

Provide some appeal mechanism. Today, virtually every employee of every organization has an appeal mechanism he can use to contest a perceived unfair appraisal—the legal system. Since employees do in fact have a way to challenge unfair appraisals, providing them with an internal means to appeal what they believe to be an unfair performance appraisal without having to go outside the organization can be a cheap form of insurance against unnecessary lawsuits.

One immediate appeal mechanism simply involves allowing the individual who believes himself to be the victim of an inaccurate appraisal to state his side of the story as a formal part of the record. Most appraisal forms contain a space for employee comments. Employees should be encouraged to use it.

Hot Tip

If the employee wants to submit a statement to be appended to the appraisal to provide a counterbalancing argument to assessments made in the formal appraisal itself, don't deny the person the right to do so. Frequently serious problems can be headed off completely if the manager says, "I'm sorry we don't see eye to eye about this, Jack, even though we've now discussed it in some detail. While I won't change the way I have written your appraisal, I certainly want to encourage you to write a statement to be attached to my appraisal if you genuinely feel that what I have written is not correct."

1.12   Is performance appraisal really necessary? Can't the benefits that the system provides to organizations and the people in them be obtained any other way?

Yes, performance appraisal is really necessary. And, no, there is no better way to obtain the benefits.

There are several books that argue in favor of abolishing performance appraisals altogether. But the procedures they recommend are merely workarounds; the steps they recommend to create an alternative to performance appraisal are the same ones that any effective organization will use to develop a world-class performance appraisal system.

Too many companies remain in denial about the benefits that a well-executed performance management system generates. They may articulate the importance of transforming their stale, best-effort culture into a tough-minded, results-driven one, but fail to understand that performance appraisal is the best tool available for muscle-building an organization.

Tell Me More

Some companies do appreciate just what a well-designed, forcefully managed performance management system can do to ensure the execution of organizational strategy. In 1999 I agreed to serve as the subject matter expert for a national benchmarking study of best practices in performance management that the American Productivity & Quality Center (APQC) and Linkage, Inc. were undertaking. My first task was to identify those companies that were in fact doing stellar work in performance appraisal, and then convince them to share their processes and techniques with the seventeen sponsor organizations that were ponying up $16,000 each to learn their secrets.

Identifying the companies that are performance management masters wasn't that difficult. But convincing them to reveal what they were doing? A different story. Several flatly refused. Many of America's most-admired companies just said no when offered the chance to be recognized as best-practice models in performance management.

Each one gave the same reason for declining to share their forms and procedures. They saw their performance management processes as a genuine source of competitive advantage and were unwilling to let any outsider peek. One human resources vice president put it bluntly when he turned me down: "We would no more show our performance appraisal form to a bunch of outsiders than The Coca-Cola Company would let you come in and look over the secret formula for Coke."

Organizations with world-class performance management systems do things that the also-rans don't. They insist that all managers maintain consistent, demanding standards for everyone—and they keep raising those standards. They work relentlessly to identify their highest potential managers and professionals and develop them quickly. They move marginal performers aside so they don't block the path of talent; they eliminate noncontributors swiftly. They treat their human resources departments as partners, staff them with the highest caliber talent available, and insist that they be active agents for change.

The best organizations create performance management systems that are (as Einstein said the solution to any problem should be) as simple as possible—but no simpler. They decide exactly what performance they want to encourage and what performance they want to purge. They identify the competencies that are core to the organization's overall success and demand that everybody be held accountable for performing like a master. They willingly tolerate complex, multi-page forms and a process that demands frequent meetings.

Finally, they closely link their performance appraisal system with their corporate strategy, mission statement, and vision and values, since they recognize that the performance appraisal system is the primary driver for making sure that mission and vision and strategy are achieved.

No other organizational system can provide all of the benefits that a professionally designed, well-executed performance-appraisal system can.

Chapter 2

Performance Planning

2.1 What is "performance planning"?

Performance planning is a discussion. It is the first step of an effective performance management process. Performance planning typically involves a meeting of about an hour or so between an appraiser and an appraisee. The agenda for this meeting includes four major activities:

1. Coming to agreement on the individual's key job responsibilities
2. Developing a common understanding of the goals and objectives that need to be achieved
3. Identifying the most important competencies that the individual must display in doing the job
4. Creating an appropriate individual development plan

Tell Me More

One of the primary reasons that performance appraisal discussions are so awkward is that they are conducted in a vacuum. If the manager and the individual haven't had a good discussion about requirements and expectations, if they haven't talked about goals, if they haven't had a meaningful dialogue about core competencies, then it will be impossible for the manager to honestly and ethically assess how well the individual has done in meeting those undiscussed objectives.

Performance planning is the bedrock of an effective performance management system. The performance-planning discussion gives the manager the chance to talk about her expectations and what she sees as genuinely important in the individual's job. It gives the individual a clear operating charter so that he can go about doing his job with the full certainty that he's working on the highest priority responsibilities and operating in a way that the organization expects.

The primary tool to use in the performance-planning meeting is your company's performance appraisal form. Since the form will be used months later to assess how well the individual did the job, it should be used from the start to plan the job expectations.

Some managers object that performance planning takes too much time; that people already know what the organization expects of them, and if they don't—well, just read the job description.

These managers are wrong. How much time is involved? In most cases, the discussion itself lasts about forty-five minutes to an hour. There's probably some time spent in preparation in advance of the meeting, and a little bit more time after the meeting to finish whatever paperwork is required.

That period may be the most valuable time the manager spends in "people-management" activities during the entire year. A minute devoted to planning may prevent hours spent on correcting and responding to an anguished reaction during a performance appraisal discussion (i.e., Is that what you wanted me to do? Why didn't you tell me?!).

2.2   What are the manager's responsibilities in the performance-planning phase of the process?

The manager has six primary responsibilities. Four of them you'll work on before the meeting with the individual. The other two you'll accomplish during the meeting.

Before the Meeting

1. Review the organization's mission statement, or vision and values, and your own department's goals.
2. Read the individual's job description. Think about the goals and objectives the person needs to achieve in the upcoming appraisal period.
3. Identify the most important competencies that you expect the individual to demonstrate in performing the job.
4. Determine what you consider to be fully successful performance in each area.

During the Meeting

5. Discuss and come to agreement with the individual on the most important competencies, key position responsibilities, and goals.

6. Discuss and come to agreement on the individual's development plan.

Tell Me More

Most of the work involved in effective performance planning happens in advance of the actual meeting. Before the meeting begins, the manager and the individual should each review the documents that will provide a big-picture perspective: the company's mission statement; the corporate vision and values statement, if there is one; the organization's strategic goals for the upcoming year; the department or division goals; and the individual's job description. The manager needs to think about the goals the individual needs to accomplish over the upcoming twelve months and the important competencies or behaviors the manager expects the individual to display in her performance.

If the manager hasn't already set goals for the department, the time to do it is before the planning meeting begins. Once the manager has identified goals for the whole department, he can ask each subordinate to set individual goals that help ensure that the overall department goals will be met.

Few organizations have job descriptions that would qualify as models of excellence. But no matter how good or bad your job descriptions are, they may be useful sources of data to indicate areas where the individual needs to concentrate attention over the course of the year.

During the meeting the manager will discuss the goals for the department and the company as a whole. He needs to work with the individual to set important, measurable, and meaningful goals that will help accomplish the department's and the organization's mission. Therefore it's important to walk into the meeting with some specific ideas for areas in which the individual should consider setting goals. The manager and the subordinate then review the most important parts of the individual's job and talk about which responsibilities are the most critical to success.

The goals and key responsibilities comprise the "what" of the job: the results, outcomes, or products. But just producing results isn't the complete story. The other part is the "how" of the job: the behaviors, competencies, or performance factors. Once the goals and responsibilities have been identified and reviewed, the appraiser and appraisee will need to talk about how the job will be done. If the company has identified core competencies that it expects every employee to display, reviewing these will allow the manager and the individual to identify the ones that are of particular importance in the individual's specific job. If the company hasn't formally identified competencies, then it's up to the manager to talk about what behaviors and skills and attributes she will be looking for in the individual's performance. The manager should begin the meeting having thought through how she wants the job to be done.

Along with discussing the how and the what of the job—competencies and results—they will also need to talk about how the individual's performance will be measured. The manager needs to describe what level of performance she will consider to be "fully successful." When the subordinate asks, "Boss, what will I need to do in order to get a good rating?" the manager needs to be prepared to respond.

The final premeeting preparation the manager needs to engage in is thinking about the subordinate's development needs. While creating and executing a development plan is the individual's responsibility, the manager needs to be prepared with suggestions on areas where development will have a payoff.

If the manager is well prepared, then forty-five to sixty minutes should be sufficient to discuss key responsibilities, set goals, discuss competencies, talk about how performance will be measured, and review the individual's ideas about plans for development.

2.3   What are the employee's responsibilities for performance planning?

While the manager has six important responsibilities in the planning phase of performance management, the individual actually has seven. Again, most of the responsibilities involve activities that happen before the actual meeting.

Before the Meeting

1. Review the organization's mission statement and your own department's goals.
2. Review your job description and determine your critical responsibilities.
3. Think about your job and identify the most important goals you feel you should accomplish in the upcoming appraisal period.
4. Think about what you consider to be fully successful performance in each area.

During the Meeting

5. Discuss and come to agreement with your appraiser on the most important competencies for your job, key position responsibilities, and goals.
6. Discuss and come to agreement on your personal development plans.
7. Make full notes on a working copy of the performance appraisal form. Keep the original of the form and give a copy to the appraiser.

Tell Me More

Before the meeting the individual should do the same kind of advance planning that the manager is expected to do: Think about what the most important job responsibilities are, identify some possible goals for review during the planning session, consider the important competencies required for success in the job, and think about how job performance will be measured. But there is one area that the individual has primary responsibility for: development planning.

Before the meeting the individual needs to think about his or her future goals and the development efforts that it will take to reach them. While the manager bears most of the responsibility for identifying the goals, responsibilities, and competencies he expects from the individual, the individual is the prime mover in identifying developmental areas and needs.

In addition to identifying the general area where developmental attention will be paid in the next twelve months, the individual should also think about the resources that will be needed to complete the plan.

In the meeting, both the manager and the individual will work together to come to understanding and agreement on the critical goals and responsibilities, the competencies, and the individual's development plans for the upcoming year. The best tool to use to record all of these agreements and understandings is the performance appraisal form itself. The individual should use a blank copy of the form and make notes on the goals, competencies, and responsibilities that she will be held accountable for over the course of the year. When the meeting is over, the individual should make a copy of the form with all of the notes and send it to the appraiser. In that way, both parties to the performance transaction will have a full record of the expectations.

2.4   When is the best time to set and review expectations?

The best time is a week or two after you have completed the performance appraisal meeting when you reviewed the official performance appraisal and discussed the person's performance during the preceding year.

Tell Me More

Ideally, every manager should close every performance appraisal discussion by saying something like, "Jane, I think we've had a really good discussion today. Over the next week or two, I'd like you to consider all the things we've discussed and think about what you will be doing in the next twelve months. I'd like you to write down the goals that you feel you should achieve next year and what the most important responsibilities of your job will be. Think about the competencies and behaviors that will be important in meeting all of your responsibilities successfully. And give some thought to your development plans for next year, too. Let's get back together in a week or two and spend an hour planning what you'll be doing over the next twelve months."

To repeat, the ideal time for the performance-planning meeting is a week or two after the previous year's performance appraisal discussion. The subjects will still be timely and the information will be easily available. But an effective performance-planning discussion can be held at any time—there doesn't need to be any other reason for scheduling a planning discussion than the manager's desire to help subordinates succeed in understanding and meeting their job responsibilities.

2.5   I have never held a performance-planning meeting. How do I get the planning meeting off to a good start?

Start by making sure you're fully prepared. Have all of the materials available that you will need: a copy of the employee's job description, the goals that you have set for your department, your notes on ideas for goals that the employee might set, the company's mission statement and similar documents, and—most important—a blank copy of your company's performance appraisal form.

Tell Me More

Open the meeting by communicating your belief about the importance of setting goals and ensuring a common understanding about performance expectations.

You might start by saying something like this:

> Thanks for coming in today, Sally. I want us to spend the next hour or so talking about what you're going to be doing over the course of the next twelve months.
>
> I want us to make sure that we both have the same understanding about what the most important parts of your job are and what goals you're going to accomplish this year. I also want to talk about how you're going to go about doing your job—the skills or competencies that are going to be important in your job performance.
>
> As we're talking about these things, we should talk, too, about how your performance is going to be measured. In that way we'll both be using the same yardsticks so there won't be any surprises when I do your performance appraisal at the end of the year.
>
> I'd also like to hear your ideas about your development plan for the upcoming year.
>
> I'd like you to keep track of all the things we talk about. Here's a blank copy of our performance appraisal form. Why don't you take your notes on it ands then make a copy of it for me after the meeting. To start, why don't we walk through the appraisal form so we see exactly how I'm going to evaluate your performance twelve months from now . . .

The opening few minutes set the tone for the entire meeting. If you begin by talking about the importance of making sure that you and the individual have a clear understanding of exactly what the job requires, it's likely you'll have a highly successful planning discussion.

2.6   What is the difference between "results" and "behaviors"?

Results include actual job outputs, countable products, measurable outcomes and accomplishments, and objectives achieved. Results deal with what the person achieved.

Behaviors include competencies, skills, expertise and proficiencies, the individual's adherence to organizational values, and the person's personal style, manner, and approach. Behaviors deal with how the person went about doing the job. The following chart will explain the difference:

Element	Focus
Results	**WHAT** the individual achieved Actual job outputs Countable results Measurable outcomes and accomplishments Objectives achieved QQCT (Quantity/Quality/Cost/Timeliness)
Behaviors	**How** the individual performed Adherence to organizational values Competencies/performance factors Traits/attributes/characteristics/ proficiencies Personal style, manner, and approach KASH (Knowledge/Attitudes/Skills/Habits)

Tell Me More

Job performance is a function of two different things: what the person accomplishes and how the person goes about doing the job. Probably all of us have encountered people who were excellent at one and failures at the other. Consider the high-pressure salesman who achieves quota by making unrealistic promises, badgering prospects into submission, and lying about his competitors' products. Great results, unacceptable behaviors. Or consider the computer programmer who works long hours, reads all of the technical journals, takes advanced classes, but can't write code that operates properly. She exhibits all of the right behaviors but she doesn't deliver the results.

For an organization to be successful, both behaviors and results are important. People have to get the job done, deliver the goods, bring home the bacon—results. And they have to do that job in a way that reflects the organization's expectations about how team members will act toward each other and outsiders—behaviors.

Hot Tip

Which is more important —behaviors or results? Although the answer varies from one organization to another (and from one individual to another), most organizations agree that a greater emphasis needs to be placed on results. In examining the performance appraisal forms from many organizations that provide for weighing different parts of the performance evaluation to determine a final appraisal rating, most of them put about two-thirds of the weight on the results the individual achieved.

2.7   How do you determine someone's key job responsibilities?

Job descriptions should provide a lot of help in determining the key responsibilities of a job but they rarely do. Too often, however, job descriptions are written in very general ways to serve many different purposes: recruitment, compensation, legal requirements, etc. As a result, they sometimes provide little information that is useful for performance management purposes.

The best way to determine the key responsibilities of a job is to start by identifying the "big rocks" of the job. The big rocks of a job are not the day-to-day tasks and chores, duties and assignments that consume all of the hours that we spend on the job. Those things are our activities.

The big rocks of the job are the major responsibilities—the reasons that we do all those tasks and chores. We engage in all of our daily activities because there are things that we are responsible for.

Tell Me More

Consider what might be the most familiar and easily understood position in an organization: the secretary or administrative assistant. The secretary is involved in a constantly changing series of tasks and mini-projects. If we watched a secretary during the course of a day's work, we would see her engage in dozens of different activities. But there are only a small number of key responsibilities or big rocks in the secretary's job. The key responsibility list might include the following items:

- Prepare documents.
- Handle faxes and copies.
- Manage the mail.
- Make travel arrangements.
- Manage information.
- Greet visitors to the office.

When you look at the list, you'll notice a few things. First, it's short. No matter what the job, there aren't all that many big rocks—major responsibilities. While people are busy doing dozens of different things during any given day, only a small number of genuinely important results are expected from the position. Five, six, or maybe seven big rocks will be sufficient to cover all of the important responsibilities in most jobs.

Second, each item is stated succinctly. There are no elaborate descriptions of the activities or the conditions under which the job is done. They are the most fundamental and uncomplicated statements of the essential responsibilities of the job. In every case the statements are simply a noun and a verb.

Third, there's no overlap. There is no connection among the various "big rocks." They are all separate and independent accountabilities. Each one refers to a discrete and separate area.

Fourth, the list includes only responsibilities, not competencies. It focuses on the outcomes of the job, not on the way the secretary goes about achieving those outcomes. Thus, there is no big rock labeled "effective communications" or "good interpersonal skills," or "friendly demeanor." Those things, if they're important, will be measured in the competencies section of the performance appraisal form.

Finally, there are no references to the quality of performance. It doesn't say that the secretary manages the mail efficiently, or greets visitors warmly, or prepares documents without making any typos. The standards of performance will be developed later. Right now, all we're concerned with is what the key job responsibilities actually are, not how the individual's performance is going to be measured.

Hot Tip

For each secretary or administrative assistant working in a different department or for a different company, the "big rocks" might well vary. The focus is not on the title of the job; the focus is on the major responsibilities of the person who acts in the capacity of administrative assistant or secretary, whatever the job title may be.

The job of secretary is one that is in the administrative job family. Next, consider the big rocks in a job in the professional/technical or clinical job family: the job of a nurse. The big rocks for an RN might be:

- Provide patient care.
- Educate patients and families.
- Assess patients.
- Ensure physician satisfaction.
- Coordinate support services.
- Ensure patient satisfaction.

Again, the number of big rocks is small (even though the nurse may do dozens of tasks over the course of one shift), but the statement of each is simple (verb and noun). No quality indicators or measures are mixed in with the statements of key job responsibilities.

Take another familiar job in the professional/technical job family: the position of personnel specialist or HR manager. The list of big rocks/key responsibilities for someone holding this position might include:

- Recruit candidates.
- Counsel employees and managers.
- Administer benefit programs.
- Conduct training programs.
- Ensure legal compliance.

Finally, consider a job from the managerial/supervisory job family: engineering project manager. The big rocks in this job might be:

- Complete projects.
- Develop new approaches and innovations.
- Create long-range plans.
- Train operations and maintenance personnel.

In this case there are only four big rocks. That's good—it's better for people to have a clear concentration on achieving a small number of genuinely important responsibilities than scatter their efforts on a myriad of minor duties.

Only when the big rocks—the key responsibilities—of a job have been identified is it possible to assess how well the person is performing the job. One of the great benefits to both the manager and the individual for spending time at the beginning of the year identifying and coming to agreement on the key responsibilities of a job is that the process ensures that the individual won't spend time working in areas that the manager feels are unimportant or more properly in someone else's domain.

2.8   Some big rocks may be bigger than others; some key job responsibilities are more critical than others. How do you determine the most important items?

The easiest way to determine what the most important key responsibility in a subordinate's job is to imagine that you're having a conversation with that person. The individual asks, "Boss, what do you think the single most important part of my job is? If I were to excel in only one area, which one would you have me do my best in?"

What would you say? Whatever you would say, that's probably the most important key responsibility in the individual's job.

Now imagine that the person says to you, "Boss, I am just overloaded. I simply can't do everything that I'm supposed to do. If I had to eliminate one thing from my job, which one of my responsibilities do you feel is the least important?"

Again, what would you say? Whatever your response, it indicates the area of least importance.

One of the great advantages of spending an hour in a performance-planning discussion is that it allows the manager and the subordinate to talk about issues like this so that the individual will concentrate time and attention on those areas that have the biggest impact on the organization's success.

2.9   How do you determine a method for evaluating someone's performance in meeting their key responsibilities?

In addition to identifying what the key responsibilities of a position are, the manager and the individual need to discuss how the person's performance will be measured and evaluated.

There are four—and only four—general measures of output:

1. Quality
2. Quantity
3. Cost
4. Timeliness

Notice that the last measure is "timeliness," not "time." That's because in measuring output, it's more useful to focus on timeliness—adherence to schedule, meeting deadlines—than it is to think about clock and calendar time.

There are also two kinds of specific performance measures:

1. Quantitative
2. Descriptive

The manager and the individual will determine for each of the competencies, the goals, and the key job responsibilities how the individual's performance will be measured.

Tell Me More

In determining the way the individual's performance will be measured, start by identifying which of the four general measures of output are the most important. Is the most critical indicator of success the number of units produced? Or is the quality of the finished product the primary concern? Or is getting the job done at the lowest possible cost the most important thing? Or is it meeting the schedule?

It's likely that more than one output measure is important. That's good—the more measures you have of performance, the more accurate and valid the assessment of performance is likely to be.

Then ask yourself how you'll determine how well the job has been done. What will be your sources of information? How will you find out how many sales calls Mary actually made? What will tell you whether the deadline was met or missed? How will you know that the products Cindy produces are of high quality? And exactly what does "high quality" mean?

If the key issue is quantity, it should be fairly easy to find numerical measures that will indicate production. Numerical measures will also be easy to find when the issue is cost or timeliness. But how do you evaluate quality when there doesn't seem to be anything to count?

Start by looking for numerical indicators that will tell you about the quality of the performance. But, remember, valid quantitative, numerical measures of quality are frequently difficult to assess. How do you evaluate the quality of a pianist's performance? It is not the number of notes struck. How do you evaluate the quality of a priest's work? It is not the number of confessions heard (though one valid measure might be the number of souls accepted into heaven, but we don't have access to the data).

Too often, the search for quantitative, numerical, countable measures of quality is fruitless, and we end up using bogus measures simply because they are easily quantifiable. For example, it would be a mistake to evaluate the quality of a programmer's performance based on the number of lines of code she writes. The critical determinant of quality programming is the ability to write elegant and parsimonious code. Likewise, the quality of a linguist or translator's performance should not be evaluated by the number of words translated. What the job requires is the ability to capture nuance; simply counting the words the linguist translates provides no indicator of that rare skill.

Particularly when we are assessing the quality of an individual's performance, the measures that are most appropriate are not quantitative but descriptive. We may find little to count, but a qualified judge can accurately describe the quality of the performance.

2.10   Descriptive measures seem subjective. Don't we have to be objective when we evaluate someone's performance?

Of course we must be objective. But what do the words *objective* and *subjective* actually mean? *The American Heritage Dictionary of the English Language* provides illuminating definitions:

> **ob-jec-tive** (ob-j· k't· v) adjective
> **1:** Of or having to do with a material object.
> **2:** Having actual existence or reality.
> **3 a:** Uninfluenced by emotions or personal prejudices: *an objective critic* **b:** Based on observable phenomena; presented factually: *an objective appraisal.*

> **sub-jec-tive** (sub-j· k't· v) adjective *Abbr.* subj.
> **1 a:** Proceeding from or taking place within a person's mind such as to be unaffected by the external world **b:** Particular to a given person; personal: *subjective experience.*

2: Moodily introspective.
3: Existing only in the mind; illusory.

It is a common mistake to think that descriptions of the quality of someone's performance are subjective unless there is some number attached. This is wrong.

Tell Me More

Objectivity lies in meeting the tests provided by the dictionary definition: If the appraiser is "uninfluenced by emotions or personal prejudices," if he is "fair," if she bases her assessment on "observable phenomena" like an employee's performance and behavior which are easily observed, and presents the appraisal factually, then that performance appraisal and that appraiser are indeed objective.

But it's easy to fall victim to the myth of quantifiability: the erroneous belief that in order for an evaluation to be objective, it must involve countable units.

Consider the Winter Olympics. The winner of the downhill ski race is determined by time. The measurement tool is a stopwatch. The fastest skier wins. In ice hockey, the winning team is again determined quantitatively: The winner is the team that scores the most goals. But what about women's figure skating? What do the judges count?

The answer, of course, is that there is nothing that they can count. Based on years of experience, with a clear model of excellence, and acting with integrity, they describe the performance and then assign a number to indicate their assessment.

In the Summer Olympics, the same is true. How is the winner of the hundred-meter freestyle determined? By the clock—the one who swims the fastest wins. What about water polo? Again, it's a quantitative measure: Whoever scores the most goals wins. But now consider platform diving. What do the judges count? Again, there is nothing that they can count. Instead, they describe the performance and assign numbers to represent their judgment about its quality.

Objectivity has nothing to do with countability. As long as appraisers meet the following three tests, they are in fact objective evaluators.

1. They have a clear model of excellence.
2. They are trained and experienced.
3. They act with integrity.

Remember: What people really want to know is the boss's opinion of their work. They want "subjective" information, to misuse the term. They want the answers to the questions: Boss, how am I doing? Do I have a bright future here? Should I be concerned about how well I'm doing my job? Are you pleased with my work?

There are no countable measures to answer those questions. However, every appraiser who is trained and experienced, who has a clear model of excellence, and who acts with integrity can answer those questions without difficulty.

2.11   Where does goal setting fit into the performance-planning process?

Goal setting is one of the key elements of performance planning. In addition to identifying the key responsibilities of the individual's job and the competencies or behaviors that the organization expects everyone to display, another critical element is setting appropriate goals for the upcoming year.

When the manager and the subordinate talk about key job responsibilities, they are talking about the specific requirements of the position—the elements that might be included in a job description. But when they discuss goals, they are talking about what the individual will do in addition to simply meeting the job description demands of the position. Setting goals produces several important results:

- It forces the identification of critical success factors in the job.
- It mobilizes individual and organizational energy.
- It forces concentration on highest priority activities.
- It increases probability of success.
- It generates increases in productivity.

Tell Me More

Thinking about goals forces the individual to think about the job itself. Why does the company have this job? What should someone who is being paid to do this job accomplish? What are the most important activities that the person holding this job should engage in? These are the questions that everyone should ask regularly; setting goals and objectives forces everyone to do this at least once a year.

Goal setting mobilizes energy. If everyone in the organization is focused on a small number of important targets, then the energy of the organization is directed toward achieving strategic ends.

If goal setting isn't a part of the performance management process, then it will be easy to get caught in the activity trap—spending time on activities that don't generate a lot of return but are done because they're familiar. If we have set clearly stated and measurable goals and objectives, we are less likely to work on low-priority tasks because we will be aware of what our high-priority responsibilities are.

Goal setting increases the probability of success. Setting specific objectives, and determining what it will take for the objective to be considered successfully achieved, tends to eliminate the excuses that are often offered up for failure: I didn't know I was supposed to do that. Is that important? Why didn't you tell me so?

Hot Tip

Goal setting directly increases productivity. Research on goal-setting programs has found that companies that introduced systematic goal-setting programs enjoyed an average 39 percent increase in productivity. Interestingly, the size of the benefit varied dramatically among the companies, with the key differentiating factor being the amount of management support. In those companies where top management lent strong support to the goal-setting initiative, there was an average 57 percent increase in productivity; but in those companies where there was little top-management support, the increase was a paltry 6 percent.

2.12 How do I pick the right goals? Where should an individual look to find goals and objectives?

There are several areas that will generate ideas for possible goals:

- The organization's vision and values statement or mission statement
- Objectives from previous review period
- Critical job responsibilities
- Your boss's objectives
- Division/department plans and strategies

- Discussions with colleagues/customers/internal clients
- Organizational problems and opportunities

Tell Me More

Mission Statement. Too often companies don't make a clear connection between their mission statement or vision and values and their performance management process. The result is that employees feel that the lofty vision or mission statements are just window dressing and don't have anything to do with their day-to-day jobs. Cynicism results.

In setting objectives, the first place to look for ideas and inspiration is the organization's mission statement or vision and values statement. Reviewing these documents will suggest areas in which objectives can be set that further the company's overall mission.

Only if employees are held accountable for behaving in the way described by their organization's vision and values or mission statement in their annual performance review, will they understand that the sentiments and attitudes expressed genuinely reflect the belief of their leaders about what is really important.

Objectives from a Previous Review Period. If the individual set objectives during a prior performance review discussion, these objectives should be considered for inclusion. And if the last year's performance review pointed out any areas where improvement or development are necessary, these would be prime targets for setting goals and objectives for the upcoming review period.

Your Boss's Objectives. Including the results that one's boss considers to be important among your objectives is not only a wise political move, it also helps ensure organizational alignment of all objectives.

Division/Department Goals. The goals of the individual's division, department, or work unit may be the most important source of objectives. If objectives or strategic plans have been established at a higher level, every individual in that work unit should have objectives that support the overall plan.

Discussions with Customers and Others. Another rich source for finding important objectives is an analysis of the customers the individual serves and the products and services provided to each customer.

Everybody (not just salespeople) has customers. Your boss and your direct reports (if you have supervisory responsibility) will always be customers for your work. If you're in a staff job, the line managers you serve are also your customers. Your peers and colleagues may be customers, too.

Start by identifying who all of your customers are. They are the people to whom you provide a product or service. Then analyze what each of your customers expects of you (an easy way to discover what they want of you is to ask them). Then figure out where you could improve your products or services to better support your customers. Those will be your goals and objectives.

Problems. Finally, look at the places where the organization is experiencing problems. Probably every employee of a company can see areas where improvements can be made; where the organization, or department, or job can be more effective. These are obvious sources of objectives.

2.13 How should a goal statement be written?

Here are some suggestions on creating workable goal statements:

- Start with an action verb.
- Identify a single key result for each objective.
- Identify costs—dollars, time, materials, equipment.
- State verifiable criteria that will demonstrate that the goal has been achieved.
- Ensure that the goal is controllable by the individual.
- Determine the relative goal priorities.
- Determine how progress will be measured and how feedback will be provided and obtained.

Tell Me More

Good goal statements begin with verbs: reduce, expand, write, eliminate, increase, arrange, create, and thousands of others. Start by thinking about the action that you're going to take.

Next, identify the outcome that will be achieved as a result of the action. Here are some examples:

- Reduce the number of customer complaints by 6 percent.
- Expand the number of choices available on the dial-up program from six to eleven.
- Write an instructional manual on the Associated brand armature.

- Eliminate one level of management in the Tyrone division.
- Increase customer satisfaction.
- Arrange three alternative distribution methods for the Ashford water purifier.
- Create an Internet-based applicant tracking system.

The sample objectives are good starts, but they're not ready for prime time yet. Next, consider whether there are any constraints or restrictions that must be met in meeting the goals. It may be that you want to "eliminate one level of management in the Tyrone division *without adversely affecting employee morale.*" You may need to "write an instructional manual on the Associated brand armature *within ninety days prior to its public release.*"

Red Flag

Be cautious of tasks or activities masquerading as goals. For example, a directive to "make ten calls on prospective clients" might seem like a reasonably well-stated goal, but it's actually an activity. What is the outcome of these calls? That's what the goal should focus on. Be careful not to use measures like "number of training programs attended." Instead, focus on what the individual did differently as a result of attending the training programs. Concentrate on the results of the behaviors, not the behaviors themselves.

How will you know that the objective has been achieved? Some of the sample goals have their measures already identified: "Reduce the number of customer complaints by 6 percent" and "Expand the number of choices available on the dial-up program from six to eleven." Others need to have measures added: "Increase customer satisfaction *by increasing the number of repeat customers by 4 percent and decreasing customer returns by 12 percent.*"

Note that the instructions do not require the objective-setter to find numerical measures to assess how well the objective has been met. Instead, they direct the individual to seek verifiable criteria that will demonstrate that the goal has been achieved. For some goals the numeric measures may be unavailable. Consider this goal: "Design a waiting room environment that creates a feeling in patients of professional excellence and personal concern." There may be no quantitative measures to evaluate the individual's performance, but that doesn't mean that measures themselves are nonexistent. The measures in this case are factors such as reduced patient anxiety reported by physicians and the creation of a "relaxed mood among patients in the waiting room, as judged by senior staffers."

Numbers are easy to verify. That is why quantitative, countable, numeric measures are better than descriptive ones—they are easier to verify. However, when assessing the quality of an individual's performance, quantifiable measures are often scarce, and descriptive measures are sufficient.

Red Flag

Sometimes in the quest for numerical, quantifiable goals, people end up measuring things that aren't important or produce unintended consequences. A goal of "answering all calls in three rings or fewer" isn't nearly as important as "presenting a genuinely gracious telephone experience."

Note the goal statement that says: "Ensure that the goal is controllable by the individual." It is difficult to hold people accountable for results that are outside their control. While total control may be absent, individuals frequently have a great deal of influence over achievement of an objective. This is particularly true in dealing with high-level, sophisticated jobs. It is appropriate for the manager to say to the individual, "Jack, I know you may not have total control over this outcome. However, in a job like this you do have a lot of influence and it is important to have someone in this position who can deliver the goods."

Not all goals and objectives are equally important. That's why it's wise to indicate the relative importance of various goals. Some organizations require a formal allocation of one hundred points to all of the goals that are set; others use an A-B-C system. Regardless of whether your company requires formal weighting of goals (most don't), be sure to discuss the relative importance of the different goals during the performance-planning meeting.

2.14 What are SMART objectives?

SMART is an acronym for the five components of an effective goal. An effective goal should be:

Specific
Measurable
Attainable
Result-focused
Time-oriented

Tell Me More

The inherent advice contained in SMART—that an objective be specific, measurable, attainable, result-focused, and time-oriented—is certainly good advice. Keep in mind, however, that all SMART offers is a test. Once an objective has been written down on paper, it is a test to tell whether it has been structured properly. It gives you no information at all about whether a goal is important or worth setting.

Red Flag

Consider an objective that states: "Reduce salary costs by terminating 10 percent of all employees over age forty by June 1, 2003." It certainly seems to meet the SMART test. But is it smart? Is it wise to lay these people off? Will the company's reputation and ability to compete effectively be enhanced by dumping the most experienced 10 percent of the staff? SMART doesn't give you a clue—the objective as it's written meets all the SMART tests. But it's likely that the person who wrote that foolish SMART objective will receive a neck-snappingly rapid legal education.

2.15   How high should I set my performance expectations?

How hard should the goals be? Should I define in advance what it will take to get a superior rating or should I simply describe what will qualify as fully successful? Should I set my objectives at the level that I need the job to be performed, or should I set them based on what I believe the employee is capable of delivering? Should I build some real stretch into my expectations? And just what is a "stretch objective," anyway?

These are some of the most difficult questions managers have to grapple with in planning the performance of their subordinates.

The easiest of these questions deals with whether the manager should identify in advance what it will take for a subordinate to get a superior performance appraisal rating. The answer is no.

What it will take to earn a "superior" or "distinguished" or "far exceeds expectations" rating simply can't be predicted in advance. There is just no way to tell in January what will be considered distinguished performance next November. Don't try. Being rated in these high performance categories usually involves unusual creativity and innovation, neither of which can be predicted a year in advance.

Instead, be absolutely clear about what it will take to earn a "fully successful" rating. If the manager is clear on what good, solid performance looks like, then the exceptions—positive and negative—will speak for themselves.

The harder issues are those that deal with just how high our expectations should be. Set your performance expectations at the level that the job needs to be done, regardless of who's doing the job. To set your expectations of one subordinate lower because you believe that his capability is modest is both insulting to him and unfair to others.

"Stretch objectives" involve doing a bit more than the individual might believe himself to be capable of. As long as they are within the bounds of possibility, people will rise to a challenge and may end up surprising themselves with what they are capable of achieving. Here is an operational test for a stretch objective: It is one where there is only a fifty-fifty chance of achieving it.

Hot Tip

Set your expectations to the demands of the job, and recognize that the demands of the job will rise every year. Top performers relish the challenge of meeting ever higher goals, and managers with high expectations are organizational talent-magnets.

No doubt it is easier to accept whatever level of effort people may choose to provide than it is to maintain tough, aggressive, and challenging expectations of everyone. But high performance flows, and high performers thrive, in an organization where high standards prevail.

2.16 What do I do if the individual disagrees with the goals I want set, or says that my standards are unreasonable, or that one of the key job responsibilities I've identified is not really part of the job?

You're the boss. You set the standards.

Tell Me More

When a difference of opinion arises in a performance-planning discussion, it's wise to begin the resolution process by listening. Ask the individual for her thoughts on the issue under discussion; inquire as to why she feels the expectations are too high or the task involved doesn't fall within her responsibilities. Restate in your own words what you understand the employee's position to be: "If I hear you right, Alice, you feel that asking for a 16 percent increase in customer satisfaction results is too high a target . . . is that correct?"

But this is not a meeting between equals. Left to their own preferences, many people will set their performance goals at levels they know they can comfortably achieve. Your job as the manager is to raise—and keep raising—the bar.

Some people won't like you if you do that. They'll complain that you're unreasonable, that you're unfair. That's okay. Your job as a manager is to bring out the best performance that each person is capable of, and sometimes that requires making people uncomfortable.

In well-managed organizations, managers are judged by the results that they produce, not by whether they are liked by all of their subordinates. Your job in the performance-planning meeting is to clearly communicate exactly what your expectations are and what it's going to take for each person to be seen as a fully successful performer when performance evaluation time rolls around. While there is always room for discussion, negotiation, and compromise, in the end, your opinion prevails.

2.17 How do I wrap up a performance-planning meeting?

Performance planning is completed when the manager and the individual have come to an understanding (ideally, an agreement) on the individual's key job responsibilities, the goals that the person will achieve over the next year, the competencies that the organization expects of its members, and the development plans the individual will pursue.

In most cases, it's best for the individual to take notes about the conversation on the performance appraisal form itself. After the meeting, the individual should make a copy of the form with all of the handwritten notes on it and send a copy to the manager. During the course of the year, the notes should be updated as projects are completed and requirements change.

But if you're dealing with a marginal performer, it's best for the manager to take the notes on the form himself. This will ensure that the manager's expectations are clearly recorded and that misunderstandings don't arise.

When the performance-planning meeting has been completed, it's time to move to the next phase of performance management—performance execution.

Chapter 3

Performance Execution

3.1   What is "performance execution"?

Once the performance-planning phase has been completed, it's time to get the job done—to execute the plan. Performance execution is the second phase of an effective performance management process. For the individual, the critical responsibility in Phase II is getting the job done—achieving the objectives. For the appraiser, there are two major responsibilities: creating the conditions that motivate, and confronting and correcting any performance problems.

In an effective performance management system, performance execution also includes a midterm review to ensure that performance is on track.

3.2   What are the manager's responsibilities in the performance execution phase?

Essentially, performance execution consists of two major responsibilities for the manager. The first is to create the conditions that motivate people to perform at an excellent level. The other is to eliminate performance problems when they arise.

The manager also has some other responsibilities in the performance execution phase of the process. They are:

- Maintaining performance records
- Updating objectives as conditions change
- Providing feedback and coaching for success
- Providing development experiences and opportunities
- Reinforcing effective behavior
- Conducting a midterm review meeting

Tell Me More

Maintaining Performance Records. Every manager has to keep track of how well the people in the department are doing. Too often, managers wait until the time for performance appraisal rolls around to discover that they can only remember what Sam or Melinda did in the last six weeks or so. That's why it's important to maintain good records of individuals' performance during the entire year.

Don't make the mistake of only keeping track of performance problems. Your records should include examples of both results and behaviors that caused you concern, as well as those that were right on target.

Updating Objectives as Conditions Change. Over the course of a year, projects will be completed and the individual will move on to the next requirement. Some projects will be altered from the expectations and requirements that were set at the start. Others will be abandoned.

It's important for the manager to regularly check on the projects, goals, and objectives that he and the individual agreed on during the performance-planning meeting. There are few situations more awkward for a manager than to have a subordinate come up and say, "We're ready to launch the new quality initiative!" when that initiative was scrapped at a higher level months before.

Every month or two, pull out the performance appraisal form with all the notes on it that the individual took during the performance-planning meeting. Read over the goals, objectives, and key responsibilities to make sure that they are as appropriate today as they were when the plan was set. If a project has been completed, note when it was finished, what the results were, and how well the individual performed. If a goal needs to be revised, get together with the individual who's responsible for it and explain the new requirements. If an objective needs to be moved up or down the priority scale, move it.

Providing Feedback and Coaching for Success. Unless someone tells them differently, most people believe that they are doing a good job and are meeting the organization's expectations. Providing routine and ongoing feedback is one of the characteristics of an effective manager.

Ideally, people should be able to track their performance independently of their manager's feedback. But good managers make a practice of consistently letting people know just what they are looking for and how their performance measures up.

Providing Developmental Experiences and Opportunities. People develop when they are presented with challenging situations, when they successfully complete the demands posed by those challenging situations, and when they reflect on what they did well and what they would do differently the next time a similar situation arises.

Managers can accelerate the development of their people by making sure that they are intentionally presented with situations that will force them to learn and to grow.

Reinforcing Effective Behavior. Years ago, in one of the first rigorous studies of what works in performance appraisal and what doesn't, General Electric discovered that criticism of an individual's performance doesn't usually result in significant performance improvement. What does work, the GE researchers found, was reinforcing the individual's strengths and encouraging him to make even more use of those skills that were particularly well developed.

Things haven't changed from that original study of fifty years ago. Building on strengths almost always provides better performance than trying to shore up weaknesses.

Of course, people problems have to be identified and resolved. But managers usually get a higher payoff from reinforcing those things that people are doing particularly well than by continually harping on their deficiencies.

Conducting a Midterm Review. While ongoing, informal feedback is essential for effective job performance, a more formal midcycle review is a powerful technique for ensuring that people's performance stays on track.

3.3   What are the employee's responsibilities in the performance execution phase?

The employee has one primary responsibility: Get the job done. There are, however, several others:

- Solicit performance feedback and coaching.
- Communicate openly with your appraiser on progress and problems in achieving objectives.
- Update objectives as conditions change.
- Complete the development plan.
- Keep track of achievements and accomplishments.
- Actively participate in the midterm review meeting.

Tell Me More

Solicit performance feedback and coaching. While the manager is responsible for providing performance feedback, the employee is also responsible for requesting it.

When Ed Koch was mayor of New York City, he would routinely walk the city's streets, buttonhole residents, and ask, "How'm I doing?" New Yorkers had little reluctance to tell Koch exactly how they thought he was doing—sometimes terrific, sometimes terrible. But Koch wanted performance feedback on a more frequent basis than he got in the city's mayoral elections every four years, so he simply went out and asked for it.

Communicate openly with your appraiser on progress and problems in achieving objectives. "No news is good news." That's not true if an organization is going to be effective. It's important for employees to let managers know when they are running into obstacles, when deadlines are in danger, when customers aren't happy. And it's important for managers to respond appropriately when bad news is announced.

Early in his career, when he had just been named plant manager of a new General Electric plastics plant, Jack Welch blew the plant up when he was experimenting with a new chemical process. A spark set off an explosion and tore the roof off the plant. No one was injured, but the damage was massive.

The next day Welch had to drive to GE's headquarters to explain himself and his mistake. "I knew I could explain why the blast went off and I had some ideas on how to fix the problem," Welch said. "But I was a nervous wreck. My confidence was shaken almost as much as the building I had destroyed."

What Welch found wasn't corporate wrath but an understanding, Socratic approach to analyzing what went wrong. His bosses' concern was with what he had learned from the experience.

"When people make mistakes the last thing they need is discipline. It's time for encouragement and confidence building," Welch later said in reflecting about the experience. "The job at this point is to restore self-confidence."

Update objectives as conditions change. The individual usually knows sooner than the manager does when an objective needs to be revised. Conditions change, other priorities interfere. Letting the manager know that a goal needs to be revised ensures the subordinate that she won't be appraised against an objective that isn't important or one that was abandoned months before.

Complete the development plan. Once the individual and the manager have agreed on the development plan, the individual is responsible for its successful execution. And just as it's important to bring any changes in objectives to the manager's attention, the individual is also responsible for letting her boss know about any significant changes in the development plan.

Keep track of achievements and accomplishments. Just as the boss is responsible for keeping track of how well people are doing and maintaining performance records, so individuals have a similar responsibility to maintain their own records of their hits and misses.

Many managers ask their subordinates to provide a list of their accomplishments at the start of the assessment phase of the performance management process. If the individual is diligent about keeping records of what he or she has accomplished over the course of the year, it will be easy to respond to this request.

Keeping good records of one's own performance is also helpful in case there is a significant difference of opinion between the individual and the manager during the performance appraisal discussion. If the individual can point to a series of genuine accomplishments that the boss has overlooked in creating the performance review, the odds go up that she may be successful in negotiating an upward change in the final rating.

Actively participate in the midterm review meeting. If the manager conducts a midcycle review, individuals can get significant benefits by being able to find out exactly how their performance is perceived before it becomes a matter of formal record (and an element of the permanent personnel record) at the time of the final year-end review.

3.4   How should I keep track of employees' performance? Should I keep a journal? And should I record day-to-day performance or just note the exceptional positive and negative events?

The method isn't all that important. What is important is having complete records of exactly how the individual did when the time for performance assessment rolls around.

The best way to make sure that you do keep track of your people's performance (once the initial energy resulting from the good intention wears off) is to use whatever record-keeping system you are using right now. How do you keep track of appointments and other important elements of the job? If you use a paper and pencil appointment calendar, start recording performance observations in it. If you routinely create and submit weekly reports, start writing a separate weekly report on your performance observations over the past five work days. It's easier to adjust an existing procedure than to create an entirely new one.

Tell Me More

An approach that is often recommended (and one that works well if the manager has the discipline to make it an ongoing part of her routine) is to create an actual performance log. A performance log is any repository for your notes and observations on the performance of the people who work for you. It might be an inexpensive spiral-bound notebook that schoolchildren use to take their notes in class. It might be a hanging file into which you place manila folders with the name of each of your subordinates written at the top. Or it might simply be a pad that you keep in a desk drawer and use exclusively for recording performance observations.

What's important is keeping written records of what people do. There are no such things as mental notes. Don't trust your memory to keep track of every employee's performance record. Use your performance log to simply jot down occasional reminders of the important activities you want to remember when it comes time for assessing the quality of that performance.

Concentrate on both positive and negative observations. The purpose of the performance log is to ensure a complete record. Besides, you're likely to find far more positive examples of performance than negative.

3.5 Should employees have access to my performance log?

No. The performance log, in whatever form you keep it, is your private and informal record of how people have done in their activities on the job.

You may find it worthwhile to have your performance log available if an employee challenges a judgment you make or a description you record in the performance appraisal. Your case is much stronger if you're able to say, "Well, George, let me get out the notes that I took at the time about the way you handled the Watson situation . . ."

Finally, if a performance appraisal you write is ever the subject of a legal or other third-party challenge, your defensibility rises if you are able to produce contemporaneous notes that led to the performance assessment in question.

3.6   How do I motivate people to deliver good performance and to correct performance problems?

The first responsibility of a manager in the performance execution phase is to create the conditions that motivate. The second is to eliminate performance problems. We'll devote all of chapter 8 to the methods and techniques that work when you're confronted with unacceptable performance. Solving people problems, however, is the unusual and infrequent occurrence. Far more common is the need to motivate people to deliver all the good efforts of which they are capable.

Motivation is internal. We cannot ourselves motivate anyone to do anything that the person does not want to do. We can force, we can coerce, we can bully and intimidate, but we can't motivate another person. We can only create the conditions that result in internal motivation.

It's not a cop-out, however, for a manager to say that she can't do anything to motivate her troops. The motivation of her troops is very dependent on whether she actually creates the conditions that lead to motivation.

Given the constant barrage of pep talks and posters, slogans, free advice, and exhortation on the topic of motivation, there should certainly be a couple of core principles of motivation that predictably work with every person, every time. Aren't there? Or are we stuck with the notion that everybody's an individual, and what's a turn-on for Sally is likely to be a turn-off for Sam?

Tell Me More

Rather than speculate about motivation, where it comes from, and how to apply it, let's gather some empirical data. Think back through all the jobs you've ever had. Bring to mind the job you had that produced the greatest feelings of motivation in you. It doesn't matter what the job was—it might be the job you have right now; it might be a job you had earlier in your career; it could even be a part-time job you had in high school. It makes no difference.

It also makes no difference what the word *motivation* means to you. However you choose to define the term is fine. Call it job satisfaction, or excitement, or enthusiasm, or a turn-on. Simply bring to mind the job that you had when you were the most motivated/satisfied/turned on.

Now that you have that high-motivation job clearly in mind, quickly jot down the factors that caused you to feel so motivated, satisfied, or turned on. If you're like most normal people, the factors you'll list are highly predictable—as are the ones that won't make your list.

On your list will appear such items as opportunities for achievement, recognition for that achievement, freedom and autonomy, challenge, the chance to learn and grow, and the work itself. What will be missing? You won't write down such important items as job security, benefits, working conditions, the quality of supervision, and the organization's policies and procedures.

It turns out that the missing link in understanding motivation is the realization that there are two different factors at work. On the one hand there are the things that motivate us, that turn us on, that generate satisfaction. On the other are those things that dissatisfy us, turn us off, demotivate us. Psychologist Fred Herzberg stated it best: Job satisfaction and job dissatisfaction are *not* flip sides of the same coin. They are entirely different coins, and the wise manager uses that insight to his or her advantage.

In short: The absence of job satisfaction is not dissatisfaction; it's simply no job satisfaction.

This is not semantic sleight-of-hand. If you eliminate all of the dissatisfiers from a job, you don't produce a worker who's happy. All you generate is somebody who mumbles, "Gee, I guess I don't have much to bitch about." This is hardly the sound of a motivated worker.

There are two separate variables at work, and if you really want a motivated workforce you have to attack on both fronts—providing satisfiers and eliminating dissatisfiers—simultaneously. Figure 3-1 illustrates the difference.

What the figure indicates is that it is possible to be both highly satisfied and highly dissatisfied simultaneously. A person can be both turned on and turned off by the same job at the same time. If the individual receives stingy benefits and labors under unsafe working conditions; if she has unpleasant interactions with her coworkers; if he serves under a nasty my-way-or-the-highway boss; if the company's policies are niggardly and job security is tenuous; then there will be much dis-

Figure 3-1. Job satisfiers and job dissatisfiers.

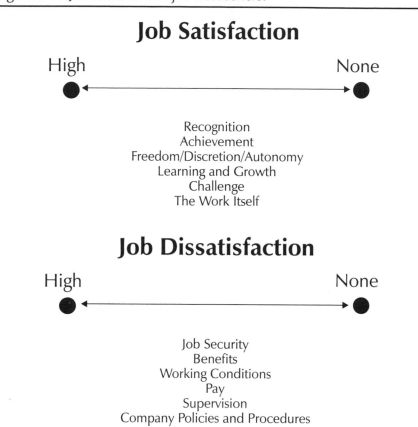

Job Satisfaction

High   None

Recognition
Achievement
Freedom/Discretion/Autonomy
Learning and Growth
Challenge
The Work Itself

Job Dissatisfaction

High   None

Job Security
Benefits
Working Conditions
Pay
Supervision
Company Policies and Procedures

Source: Grote Consulting Corporation.

satisfaction among the troops. But curing all of these distasteful conditions will not generate a cadre of turned-on high performers. It will simply eliminate all of the complaining. If people didn't like what they were doing before, they won't like it any more, even though their working conditions have improved. If the job was boring and pointless previously, granting a few extra weeks of vacation or running all the bosses through sensitivity training won't make it challenging and appealing.

A good working definition of motivation is this: Motivation represents a measurable increase in both job satisfaction and productivity. The motivated worker does his job better and likes it more than those folks who are not so motivated. What truly motivates people is the first set of factors mentioned: opportunities for achievement and accomplishment, recognition, learning and growth, discretion, and worthwhile work. Those are the items that generate strong feelings of loyalty, satisfaction, enthusiasm, and all those other things we want to see in those whose paychecks we sign.

Hot Tip

You can't get away with working exclusively on the satisfiers' scale. You have to make sure that you clean up the job environment to reduce or eliminate those things that cause people to be unhappy and quit.

3.7   What about pay? Isn't money the only thing that really motivates?

Where does money fit into this scheme?

Pay is the ringer in the motivation equation. It is the one factor that shows up as both a source of satisfaction and a source of dissatisfaction. People are dissatisfied with their pay when they feel it isn't commensurate with their efforts, is distributed inequitably, doesn't reflect the responsibilities of the job, or is out of touch with market realities. If you don't pay competitive wages, people will be unhappy and they will quit. No matter how much you raise salaries, though, you won't generate motivation and job satisfaction, because job satisfaction is a function of the content of the job.

On the other hand, if people feel that their pay reflects the quality of the contribution they are making to their organization, and is equitable with other high-talent performers inside and outside the company, and recognizes the unique contributions that they make, then pay can be a powerful source of true motivation.

Tell Me More

Look at it this way: Hire me to wash dirty dishes and pay me chicken feed and I'll be unhappy and unmotivated. But raise my wages to a princely sum and guess what—I'll still hate washing dirty dishes. But I won't complain anymore about my crummy compensation; I probably won't quit; and I may even improve my attendance record (if you pay me my now-lavish wages on an hourly basis). What you have bought with the munificent pay increase you provided me was not the presence of satisfaction. All you have bought is the absence of dissatisfaction. If you really want me to be a happy camper, you'd better change the nature of my work.

And changing the nature of the work is the true key to motivation. The message is clear: Do everything you can to mollify the generators of employee unhappiness, recognizing that no matter how big an investment you make in compensation you'll get precious little in return. All that your money will buy is the absence of dissatisfaction. Listen up: You have no choice! You must pay people competitive wages, you must provide a healthy, safe, and attractive work environment, you must give at least as good insurance policies, vacations, and retirement plans and other benefits as they could get working for the bagel joint down the street. If you don't, people will leave you and you won't be able to hire replacements. But all you'll get for the fortune you spend in this effort is a bunch of people who have to search hard for something to bitch about.

If you want genuine motivation, you've got to look at the job itself. Does the work provide people with the chance to really accomplish something? I'm not talking about the psychological trap of providing a sense of accomplishment. I don't want a sense of anything, and neither does anybody who's working for you. What we want is the opportunity for real achievement, for genuine accomplishment. Does my job allow me to do something that makes an actual difference? Do I get recognized for what I do—recognized both financially and through nonmonetary means? Do I have a lot of say in how I do my job or am I totally constricted by standard operating procedures? Can I learn and grow and develop on this job, or will I be tightening the same nut on the same bolt for the next thirty years?

The Peace Corps knows the secret. The Peace Corps generates incredible feelings of motivation among its volunteers because it provides them with jobs worth doing. The Peace Corps sticks middle-class Americans in malarial jungles and feeds them grubs and bugs. Why don't their volunteers flee? Because while they're there they have the chance to transform the lives of entire communities and populations. CARE is another sterling example. And many other not-for-profit organizations have overcome their inability to pay Wall Street wages by giving people the best jobs they might dream of. The message is clear: If you can't satisfy people's pocketbooks, then satisfy their souls. And most companies have the capability of providing soul-satisfying work.

The motivation problem that most managers face is that since they can't compete with megabucks corporations in what they pay their people, they tell themselves that even trying to motivate people is useless. They abandon all efforts and merely hope that staff will somehow develop internal generators of motivation independent of any efforts they make from the top.

3.8 What can a manager do to create the conditions that motivate?

Six techniques have a predictable effect on increasing an individual's motivation:

1. Create opportunities for achievement and accomplishment.
2. Allow people freedom, discretion, and autonomy in doing the job.
3. Provide opportunities for learning and growth.
4. Increase the amount of challenge.
5. Make sure that the work itself is inherently capable of motivation.
6. Provide recognition.

Tell Me More

Create opportunities for achievement and accomplishment. Is the job worth doing? Can the individual do anything to be proud of, or is it just the same old, same old?

The classic example of increasing opportunities for achievement involved Emery Air Freight's success in increasing the use of containers to consolidate several small packages into one large container. The company's stated goal was 95 percent utilization of containers and, while it was not precisely measured, the assumption on the part of most managers and employees was that the 95 percent goal was being achieved regularly.

One day Ed Feeney, an Emery senior manager, actually audited the operation to see what percentage of shipments that could be consolidated into single containers actually were. He was astounded at the result. Instead of 95 percent of the goal, the operation was achieving only 45 percent.

Feeney corrected the problem by providing feedback to each individual dockworker about his actual level of performance. He accomplished this by creating a simple form that required the dockworker to write the name of the shipper for each item, to note whether or not each package being processed met the requirements to be consolidated, and to indicate whether or not it actually was consolidated into a larger container. At the end of the shift, the dockworker calculated the actual percentage of those packages that were containerized against those that should have been containerized and turned the form over to his foreman. When this form was introduced nationwide, the overnight result was an increase in containerization from a national average of 45 percent to 95 percent. Not only did Emery dramatically increase its effectiveness, but the dockworkers and supervisors were given an excellent opportunity for genuine achievement.

Allow people freedom, discretion, and autonomy in doing the job. How much say do people have in deciding how they perform their jobs? Do they have any discretion or are the procedures completely specified? Can an individual exercise good judgment, or does policy dictate everything? Are employees permitted to use common sense, or is any variation from standard operating procedures punished?

A commonly reported motivational factor is the ability to operate independently, to think for oneself. Let's look at how a manager can increase the amount of discretion that a job provides.

All jobs are done in one of three different modes. Some parts of the job are done in the "do" mode. In this mode the individual has total authority—he doesn't have to get anyone's permission in advance; she isn't required to let her boss know what she's done. The individual is entirely free to act and get the job done any way he wants.

The second mode in which jobs are done is "do/report." The individual is fully free to act, but must let the boss know afterward what was done and how it went.

Finally, there's the "check/do/report" mode. Here the individual has no autonomy. Before acting, the employee must first get the boss's approval (or run it by the committee, or check with the rest of the team). Then the person can do what needs to be done, but then must report—fill out a transaction summary form, include it on the weekly report, review the transaction with the supervisor.

Figure 3-2 displays the three modes in which jobs are done. There is something disturbing about the way this triangle has been drawn. As it stands, it represents a very sick job. Can you see why?

The reason is that the way the triangle is portrayed above, the huge majority of tasks fall into the check/do/report area—the part of the

Figure 3-2. Check, do, and report triangle.

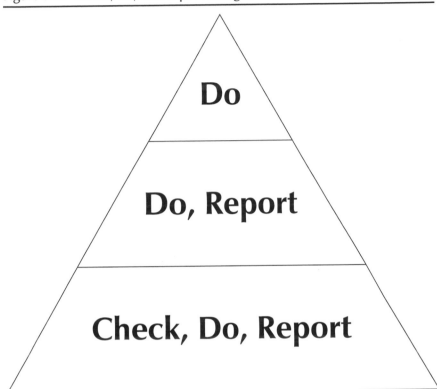

job where the individual has the least amount of discretion. A smaller number of tasks fall into the do/report portion of the triangle.

Finally, the smallest area of all is the one in which the individual has the greatest amount of autonomy: Do.

The job of the manager who wants to increase the amount of motivation people feel is to turn the triangle around; to rotate it so that the largest part of the job is in the area where the person has the most authority and the smallest part where the individual has the least amount of say in how the job is done. Figure 3-3 illustrates the way the triangle ideally should look.

How does a manager go about rotating the triangle? Start with those tasks or assignments that you routinely ask a staff member to check in with you before he undertakes the task. If you routinely approve the recommended action, this task is a good candidate for moving up from the check/do/report mode to the do/report mode. You might say, "Harry, from now on, every time a customer exception re-

Figure 3-3. Rotated check, do, and report triangle.

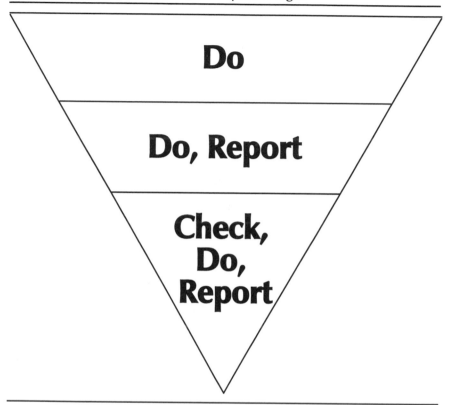

quest comes in, you can just handle it by yourself . . . you don't have to run your plan for responding to it by me any more. Of course, I'll always be available to review anything that you think is unusual, but from now on you can take care of this without checking with me." Congratulations! You have just increased the amount of authority in Harry's job.

Next, identify those assignments or activities that you regularly ask your staff members to report on to you. Look for where you routinely take no action based on their reports. Those are the candidates to move from a do/report mode to the do mode. You might say, "Louise, in the past I have always asked you to let me know as soon as you've closed out a major client record account. You won't have to advise me of that anymore—you know what you're doing and I've got confidence in your ability to do it right. Let me know of any accounts that are unusual, but the rest of them you can handle 100 percent by yourself." Again, the amount of authority in Louise's job has just been increased.

Increase the amount of challenge. When people are asked to identify the job that produced the greatest feelings of motivation or job satisfaction, one of the most frequent factors they reported is that the job provided a genuine challenge.

Where should a manager look for ways in which to increase the challenge quotient of a subordinate's job? The answer is, look to your own job.

Visualize your job as a silo. At the very top of the silo are those tasks and responsibilities that only you can do. Only you have the knowledge, the capability, the insights, and the talents to do these things at the very top of your silo. They are the ones that demand the highest talents you have . . . the ones that justify the big bucks you're getting paid.

In the middle of the silo are those tasks and activities that are genuinely important, but that you have under firm control. They may have been highly challenging at some time in the past, but today, even though their importance remains high, you do them without a great deal of difficulty.

Finally, there are those things at the bottom of the silo—the scut work that shows up in everyone's job. All of us have to fill out expense reports; no one is exempt from writing the weekly report; everybody has to take part in the fire drill. Undemanding and unchallenging, they still need to be done.

Now think about your subordinate's job. It too can be represented as a silo, just like yours. But as Figure 3-4 indicates, those items and responsibilities at the top of your subordinate's silo aren't as high as yours. Their tasks, assignments, and job requirements aren't as demanding as the ones at the top of your silo. But notice that there's no difference at the bottom of the silo. Scut work is scut work, and it doesn't matter whether it's done by the hospital's CEO or the guy who washes the bedpans.

Here's how to increase the opportunities for achievement in a subordinate's job. Find one of the tasks in the upper half of your silo and move it over to your subordinate, as shown in Figure 3-5.

Look at the diagram and answer this question: What has just happened to the importance of the task? The answer is, of course, nothing. The task has neither increased nor decreased in importance. The importance of the task is unchanged.

What has changed is the composition of the two silos. The subordi-

Figure 3-4. Silo job diagram.

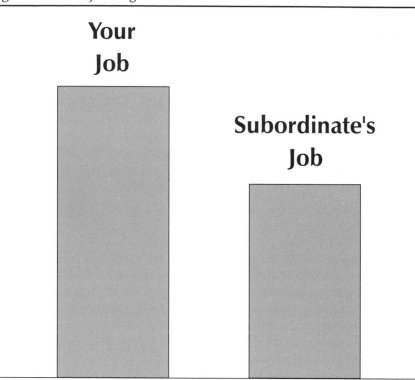

nate now has been given a very high-level, challenging responsibility—and for most people, challenging jobs are motivating jobs. The manager has also benefited. By delegating an important responsibility to a subordinate, you not only increase the amount of challenge and the chances for real achievement in your subordinate's job, you have also freed yourself to spend more time on those responsibilities that only you have the capability to perform. The name we use for this process is delegation.

But a couple things go wrong when managers attempt to delegate. First, they may become enamored of the idea of delegation and try to delegate a task at the very top of their silo—one that is beyond the subordinate's current capability to succeed at. In this case the subordinate fails and the delegation process gets a bad reputation.

The opposite problem shows up when a manager delegates a responsibility at the bottom of his silo. If a task has no motivational value for you, it's not going to have much motivational value for anybody else. The classic example is the manager who says, "Sam, you did such

Figure 3-5. Silo job diagram #2.

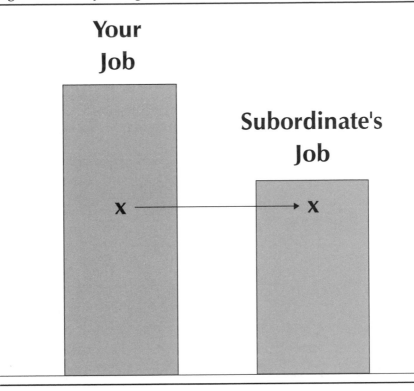

a good job of washing the dishes, I'm going to let you wash the silver-ware, too!" Washing dishes, washing silverware, there's no challenge involved here. Figure 3-6 illustrates these problems.

The biggest problem with using delegation as a motivational de-vice is that managers simply don't get the motivational benefits that delegation can provide. They part only with those responsibilities that they're glad to be rid of and hold tightly to the most enjoyable parts of their jobs. For example, the manager who prides herself on her ability to placate an irate customer will actively seek out irate customers to placate. Since she is able to do this demanding task skillfully, and since she gains a great deal of personal satisfaction from doing so, it's un-likely that she will turn the responsibility for dealing with troubled customers over to any of her subordinates who desperately need to learn the skills that she has acquired. Two unfortunate consequences result from this kind of behavior. First, talented subordinates are likely to be dissatisfied and unmotivated, since they don't get to do the chal-lenging part of the job and have their learning opportunities con-

Figure 3-6. Silo job diagram #3.

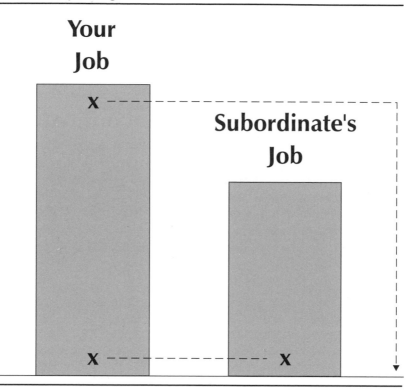

stricted. Just as bad, the manager is unlikely to be promoted to a better job, since her seniors are likely to say, "Well, we certainly can't take Sally out of that post. Nobody else in the company is able to deal with irates as well as she does. We *need* her there!"

3.9   What about recognition? Isn't recognizing an employee who's done good work an effective motivational tool?

Yes. Recognizing good performance is the single most important motivation tool managers have at their disposal. It is cheap (usually free), is universally liked, and results in an increase in desired performance.

Tell Me More

Behind this question about motivation lurks a larger issue: How do we go about changing human behavior? Motivating a person involves getting that person to decide to do more of behavior A (e.g., coming to work on time, taking an entrepreneurial approach to her work, completing reports when they are needed) and less of behavior B (e.g., coming late, doing the minimum required, missing deadlines).

What do we know for sure about human behavior? The truth is, we know precious little. But it turns out that there is one thing that we do know for sure, one thing that is highly predictive of human behavior. It is the seven-word principle that psychologist B. F. Skinner promulgated in 1936: "Behavior is a function of its consequences." Never has truth been captured more succinctly.

What Skinner meant was this: To a large extent, what people do depends on what happens to them as a result. If a person does something and the consequence is positive/rewarding/pleasant, the person will keep on doing that thing. If a person does something and discovers that the consequences are negative/punishing/distasteful, she will stop doing that thing. And if a person does something and finds out that there are no consequences—nothing at all happens—he may keep it up for a short time but eventually, to use Skinner's fancy phrase, the behavior will be extinguished.

Although making significant changes in jobs to increase their motivational value is an important long-term effort, the decision to immediately start providing recognition of good performance anytime it's encountered can get the motivational engine working fast. Acknowledging excellent work every time it appears is a wonderful way to start increasing motivation fast.

3.10 We're considering starting an employee-of-the-month program. Is this a good recognition tool?

No. Don't do it. Employee-of-the-month programs are a notoriously bad idea.

Tell Me More

The problem with employee-of-the-month programs is not so much with the concept, but with the execution. The concept is a noble one: Every month the organization will review the employee population and single out that one individual who, in the month past, has achieved some remarkable success or has otherwise performed exceptionally well. That's the theory.

In practice it doesn't quite work that way. To begin, every month the company names one winner. What does that make all of the rest of the company's employees? The answer: losers.

Another problem comes up in determining how the lucky employee will be selected each month. Will there be specific criteria, like getting the highest score on the customer satisfaction survey or bringing in the most new accounts? What will you do when, month after month, Esmerelda gets the highest score and once again qualifies as your employee-of-the-month? Pretty soon people will start to resent both the program and Esmerelda. Esmerelda will discover that her life is far more pleasant if she does a mediocre job to avoid being stigmatized as the employee-of-the-month one more time.

What if you don't have criteria and just cast about for nominations every month? With no criteria, there will be little relationship between the person earning the accolade and the quality of performance displayed. If the tangible rewards that accompany being named the monthly winner are significant (a reserved parking place close to where the CEO parks, a free dinner at a decent restaurant), it will soon devolve into a popularity contest. If there are no significant perks other than having one's name engraved on a little bronze fitting on a little wooden plaque, then it will soon become the monthly drawing of a name from a hat.

Companies and their managers rush into employee-of-the-month and other trinket programs because they seem like easy fixes, not realizing the amount of energy that it takes to make the program work effectively month after month. A program that kicks off in January will get a lot of attention through March or April. By May the program is becoming familiar. By July supervisors are unresponsive and ignore requests for nominations. And around September you'll start hearing the comments, "Is it time for that damned employee-of-the-month program again?"

Red Flag

The worst thing about an employee-of-the-month program is that it denies the supervisor's responsibility for being the primary dispenser of employee recognition. If a company has an employee-of-the-month program, then the supervisor can rationalize his failure to recognize good performance on his subordinates' part by saying, "That's the responsibility of the employee-of-the-month program."

To test whether the employee-of-the-month concept is really a valid idea, test it yourself. Then next time you're in an office, restaurant, or hotel that proudly posts their plaque of employees of the month, locate one of the recipients and ask that person, "What did you actually do to win the employee of the month award?" Most of the time the person will simply respond, "I have no idea."

3.11   Do people need praise every time they do a good job?

No. If you recognized good performance every time someone did something right, you'd have no time to do anything else, and they would get bored by it.

The key is to make the recognition you provide commensurate with the quality of the job that was done. As the person's skills increase, the quality of job performance must also increase before recognition follows.

Tell Me More

Consider one of the most elementary of human behaviors: walking. The parents of an infant make a major production over encouraging their baby to walk. When the baby takes his very first step, the parents celebrate the occasion, haul out the video camera, and shower the baby with kisses and hugs. Kisses and hugs from Mom and Dad are powerful reinforcers when you're twelve months old. The baby learns that all he has to do is take a wobbly step or two, and the love starts flowing.

But quickly, Mom and Dad raise the stakes. Just one baby step isn't enough to bring on the love fest. Now Junior has to walk all the way across the room. But when he does, the reinforcement is there again.

Gradually the child learns to walk. Reinforcement/recognition is the powerful motivator behind the child's acquisition and use of the new skill. But once he's got it, he's going to have to execute a pas de deux or run a hundred-yard dash in nine flat to get any further reinforcement for his walking ability.

The message? Use reinforcement a lot when someone is learning a new job or acquiring an unfamiliar skill. Use a lot more when someone does something remarkably well. But taper off the recognition once the skill has been acquired—you don't really expect to be praised for tying your own shoes anymore, do you?

3.12   I don't have a budget for awards to recognize people. How can I recognize their good performance if I can't demonstrate financially that we appreciate good work?

Money is only one of your options in recognizing good performance. The most important concept about recognition comes directly from the word itself—"to recognize." When you recognize something, you are aware of it, you are not ignoring it, you're paying attention to it. That is the heart of recognition—letting people know that you are aware that they performed well and that you appreciate their good work.

Recognition can be symbolized in many ways, but it always starts with awareness.

Tell Me More

Managers have a huge supply of tools available to them to use in recognizing good performance. Let's take a look at some that are easily available, that don't cost very much money, and that everyone seems to like:

- Saying a simple and sincere "Thank you"
- Asking an employee's advice about how to improve the department's effectiveness
- Eating lunch together
- Giving an employee a more desirable job assignment
- Writing your boss a memo about the great job she did
- Letting an employee take an extended lunch
- Forwarding a newspaper or magazine article to a subordinate
- Giving a subordinate an advance copy of a new company brochure or advertisement
- Arranging for an employee to be given a supply of business cards
- Writing a quick "Thanks!" on a Post-it Note and sticking it on a colleague's phone
- Introducing an employee to a visitor and explaining how her work contributes to the company's success
- Making a ridiculous plaque and conducting a silly presentation ceremony
- Writing the employee a favorable memo and sending a copy to her personnel file

Notice that many of the above items actually use the job as a motivator. Allowing a person to have a more desirable job assignment, or arranging for an individual to get his own business cards, or permitting an employee her choice of tasks to do, can be more valuable than any trinket.

But the most important motivator is the words that come out of your mouth. Saying "Thanks" or "Well Done!" or "I really appreciate that" is a powerful source of recognition and reinforcement.

3.13   Is recognition just a matter of heaping on the praise?

No. In fact, praise has very little to do with true recognition of good performance. Have you ever noticed how people react to praise? Not very graciously, most of the time.

Praise a house or a garden and its owner hastens to point out its defects; praise an employee for a project and he downplays his role; praise a child and he digs in his toes. The typical responses to praise are such rejoinders as: "Oh, it was nothing. It was just luck. You're just saying that. Well, I do the best I can. I like yours, too."

Tell Me More

Bosses are constantly told that the way to motivate the troops is to tell 'em what a great job they're doing. Give 'em some recognition, the management experts urge, a little positive feedback. But check the reaction of those on the receiving end of this blarney and ask yourself if it's really a motivator.

Why do people react to praise with such defensiveness? In part it may be modesty, but mostly the reason is that in praise there is threat, there's something we must defend against. What rankles us about praise is not that we're being evaluated positively, but that we're being evaluated at all. When a person praises us, it is clear that he is sitting in judgment. We become uneasy when we realize that someone is giving us a grade.

Praise serves to maintain status differences. It reminds one person that another is capable of sitting in judgment. When the work of a high-status person is praised by a low-status person, it's usually taken as presumptuous or insulting. Imagine a layman telling Picasso, "You know, you're really a very good painter . . . "

We also sugarcoat bad news or criticism with praise and turn it into psychological candy. We use the sandwich technique. Start with a bit of praise ("You're doing a great job, Fosdick, a great job . . ."). Then let him have it ("But there are a few things we need to talk about . . ."). Finally, having given him both barrels, wrap it up with just a little more plastic applause ("Keep up the good work, Fosdick"). No wonder Fosdick winces when he's told he's doing well.

But people are always fishing for compliments and complaining about being underappreciated by the boss. We live in a constant state of stroke-deprivation. We remember for years the kind things others have said. How can we use praise well?

The trick is to describe and report, not to evaluate and judge. We're uncomfortable being praised because someone is judging us, but we're entirely at ease when we're told of the positive reaction our accomplishment produces in another. It's the difference between telling Mr. Picasso that he's a pretty good painter, and explaining that seeing a simple daisy he painted made us smell a whole bouquet of flowers.

Start by making your comments direct and specific. Tell the individual exactly what it is that he or she has done that you like. Then say why you like it. Instead of judging the worth or value of the other person, talk about the impact of what it is they've done. "I really appreciate your staying late last night, Mary. It allowed me to finish up my report well in advance of the deadline." "That last client presentation was great, Fred. Everyone followed closely and you provoked a lot of important questions."

Finally—and here's the real secret to making verbal recognition work for you—immediately ask a question such as, "Did you have to make special arrangements?" or "How did you learn to be so relaxed in front of a group?"

The flaw in praise is often thought to be a lack of sincerity. But sincerity has little to do with it. State the compliment for the specific thing the individual has done, justify it, ask a question, and the sincerity will take care of itself.

3.14   How do I actually use recognition? Is there more to it than just saying, "Thanks . . . nice job"?

Yes, there is more to it, but not much more.

The most important—and most ignored—requirement to make

recognition an effective motivational tool is the notion of earned or contingent recognition. If we want to make the recognition we provide actually have a motivational stimulus, the recognition that the individual receives must be contingent on that person's having done something that is worthy of being recognized. If we just recognize people as a nice human relations tactic, then our recognition efforts will have no motivational value at all.

Tell Me More

Too often, the reason that recognition fails to generate motivation (measurable increases in job satisfaction and job performance) is that the recognition effort isn't connected to anything the person has done. For example, consider the manager who makes a point of greeting each of her employees with a friendly remark every morning. She sends each staff member a card on the person's birthday and regularly springs for a Friday all-hands pizza party. She makes a point of making herself available to talk any time a staff member has a concern and goes out of her way to approve requests for schedule changes and training program participation. With all that good stuff she's providing, she should have a highly motivated staff, right?

Not necessarily. What's missing here is the notion of contingent recognition. Regardless of the quality of Daniel's work, he's greeted warmly every morning as he enters the office. Whether Samantha's done a good job or a bad job, her request for training is approved. The office star and the office goof-off are both invited to the pizza party. There's no connection between employee performance and the good things that happen at the office. As a result, all these good things the supervisor does have no motivational value.

Don't get me wrong. I'm not arguing that a manager shouldn't create an office environment where people feel welcomed and appreciated. Doing so will remove a source of dissatisfaction. But it won't motivate people to work harder or do better, since no matter how hard they work the same pleasant outcomes are provided.

What is needed for recognition to work is for the good things that happen to be connected to the good job that the person does. If the good things a manager does for employees are done on a random basis, then what you will get back is random behavior. Recognition must be tightly connected with job performance if it's going to affect job performance.

3.15   Won't some people—the better performers—end up getting more recognition than others who don't perform as well? Isn't that discriminatory?

Yes, it is discriminatory. If some people do better work than others do, then they should get more recognition. The better, more productive employees will get more freedom to act and more Post-its saying "Thanks" stuck to their computer monitors. They will be allowed more flexibility in their schedules and get first choice when interesting new projects arise. And they will have earned these advantages because they make a more valuable contribution to the organization. It's okay to discriminate on the basis of performance.

Tell Me More

There is a pernicious myth in organizations that says that everyone has to be treated the same—that you can't do something for one employee without doing it for all employees. That is not true. What the law prohibits is treating people differently based on factors that have nothing to do with their job performance: race, age, sex, national origin, and so on. But there is no law prohibiting organizations from treating people differently based on the quality of their work.

There are two kinds of rewards in organizational life: the obligatory rewards and the discretionary rewards. Obligatory rewards are those things that everyone is entitled to, regardless of how well they do their jobs. Some examples: a paycheck that arrives when it's due and does not bounce, a clean, safe, and healthy work environment, equal access to the company's benefit plans, an environment free of any form of harassment.

No manager can diddle with the obligatory rewards the organization offers in an attempt to raise motivation. He can't double Mary's insurance reimbursement from having her appendix out because she did a particularly good job in bringing in new accounts, nor can he deny Fred's legitimate tuition reimbursement request because Fred has been late to work too often. The obligatory rewards have to be provided exactly according to policy until the day that the employee quits, retires, is fired, or dies.

Discretionary rewards are different, though. Here the manager is allowed to exercise great control over who gets what. He can decide that because Mary did such a great job in building new accounts he's going to allow her to serve on the annual event committee instead of

Fred. He can also refuse to allow Fred time off to attend the marketing society's convention until his attendance record improves. He is not obliged to allow Fred to attend; giving Fred permission is at his discretion.

The wise manager actively uses discrimination in doling out recognition, making sure that high performers get a lot of the discretionary rewards and that poorer performers get proportionately less.

3.16 Won't people complain when I deliberately treat some people better than others? Won't I be accused of favoritism?

Yes, they will complain. Yes, you will be accused of favoritism. That's okay.

Consider where the complaints are coming from—the poorer performers. If you treat everyone exactly alike, regardless of performance, you will also get complaints. But this time those complaints will originate with your best workers, the ones you least want to provoke complaints from.

The manager who strives to make everyone happy and satisfied is pursuing a foolish course. The manager's job is to make sure that some people—the better performers—are very happy and very satisfied. And if the poorer performers feel that that's unfair, all the manager needs to do is explain to them what they need to do to move up into the realm of the higher performers.

The primary requirement for successful performance management is courage. Being a good manager requires some skills, but most people have the capability to learn those skills and apply them reasonably well. What ordinary managers lack is courage: the courage to accept that some people do perform better than others do, and to use discretion in handing out formal and informal rewards.

Chapter 4

Performance Assessment

4.1   What is "performance assessment"?

Performance assessment is the third phase of an effective performance appraisal system. Basically, performance assessment involves evaluating just how good a job the individual has done and filling out the appraisal form.

Tell Me More

Too often, people think that performance appraisal is an event—a once-a-year drill required by the personnel department in which the manager fills out the form and then uses it to give feedback and justify raises.

That's wrong. But that notion is so common, it causes a lot of people to be skeptical of performance appraisal.

Evaluating someone's performance is one of the last activities in an effective appraisal system, not one of the first. As previously discussed, the process should start with performance planning, the hour-long conversation between the manager and the individual in which they discuss the goals, competencies, objectives, and key job responsibilities. The next phase of an effective performance management system is performance execution. For the individual this involves getting the job done; for the manager it means creating the conditions that motivate and solving performance problems.

Managers often complain that evaluating someone's performance is difficult. The reason that they find it difficult is usually that they haven't done a good job of performance planning at the beginning of the year. If a manager hasn't held a planning discussion at that time, it's difficult to evaluate performance at the end of the year.

4.2 What are the manager's responsibilities for performance assessment?

The manager has eight primary responsibilities in the performance assessment phase:

1. Review the original list of competencies, goals, objectives, and key position responsibilities.
2. Prepare a preliminary assessment of the employee's performance over the entire year.
3. Review the individual's list of accomplishments and the self-appraisal.
4. Prepare your final assessment of the employee's performance.
5. Write the official performance appraisal using the appraisal form.
6. Review the appraisal with your manager and obtain concurrence.
7. Determine any revisions needed to the employee's key position responsibilities, goals, objectives, competencies, and development plans for the next appraisal period.
8. Prepare for the performance review meeting.

Tell Me More

Review the original list of competencies, goals, objectives, and key position responsibilities. At the beginning of the year, the manager and the individual discussed the competencies the individual would be expected to display in going about her job responsibilities and the goals and objectives to be achieved. Ideally, the subordinate would have recorded the notes from this discussion on a blank copy of the appraisal form and then made a copy for the manager afterward. This document serves, then, as the charter under which the subordinate operates during the course of the year, secure in the knowledge that she's doing the job as the organization expects it done and concentrating on the highest priorities.

At the end of the year, the manager's first step is to get out that performance appraisal form with the notes on it. Ideally, it has been updated and revised over the course of the year with notes on projects completed and with new objectives added. But even if it hasn't been revised, reviewing the form is still the best way to start the assessment process—by looking at what the two parties agreed on at the beginning of the year.

Prepare a preliminary assessment of the employee's performance over the entire year. Before you write the official appraisal, it's a good idea to take a blank copy of the form and make some preliminary notes. Whether you're working with a paper and pencil process or drafting the appraisal on your computer, begin by jotting down some rough notes on areas where you recall the person's performance as particularly strong or weak. Identify those assessments required by the form that you don't have information immediately available for. Draft some very preliminary conclusions to start your thinking process about the entire evaluation.

Review the individual's list of accomplishments and the self-appraisal. It's a good idea to ask each individual whose performance you'll be evaluating to send you a list of their most important accomplishments and achievements over the course of the year. In addition to the list of accomplishments, you may also ask the individual to complete a full self-appraisal using a blank copy of the form.

Prepare your final assessment of the employee's performance, and write the official performance appraisal using the appraisal form. This is the most important activity in the performance assessment phase of performance appraisal. Following the recommendations and suggestions in this chapter will allow you to complete this responsibility at a level that anyone assessing your performance would describe as "far exceeds expectations."

Review the appraisal with your manager and obtain concurrence. Whether or not your company requires you to get your boss's sign-off on an appraisal before you discuss it with an individual, it's a good idea to review any appraisal with your immediate supervisor before you conduct the performance appraisal discussion.

Determine any revisions needed to employee's key position responsibilities, goals, objectives, competencies, and development plans for the next appraisal period. Part of the performance appraisal meeting will be historical—looking back on the individual's performance over the past twelve months. Another part will focus on the future—what needs to be done differently during the next twelve months. Although it's a good idea to conduct a separate performance-planning discussion a week or two after the performance appraisal conversation, during the meeting it's wise to be prepared to talk about changes that you will expect in the person's performance next year.

Prepare for the performance review meeting. Performance appraisal discussions are some of the most sensitive and demanding of all meetings that managers are involved in. The better job that you do to prepare, the more comfortable and effective the discussion will be.

4.3   What are the employee's responsibilities in the performance assessment phase?

Both the manager and the individual have responsibilities in the performance assessment phase of the process, just as they do in each of the other phases. The individual has six key responsibilities:

1. Review your personal performance over the year.
2. Assess your performance and accomplishments against the development plan.
3. Prepare a list of your accomplishments and achievements and send it to your appraiser.
4. Write a self-appraisal using the appraisal form.
5. Consider any revisions needed to your key position responsibilities, goals, objectives, competencies, and development plans for the next performance review cycle.
6. Prepare for the performance review meeting.

Tell Me More

Review your personal performance over the year. Performance appraisal is not exclusively the responsibility of the manager. Each person regularly needs to ask himself the question, "How am I doing?" The advantage of a formal performance appraisal system is that it forces this beneficial review on at least an annual basis.

Assess your performance and accomplishments against the development plan. The manager's assessment concentrates on how well the individual did in meeting job responsibilities—goals, objectives, competencies. The individual needs to do the same. Another area for the individual to closely focus on is how well she did in carrying out the development plans that were made at the start of the year.

Prepare a list of your accomplishments and achievements and send it to your appraiser. Whether or not the manager requests the individual to write an accomplishments list, the wise individual in every organization always keeps track of her major successes and achievements (and makes sure that the manager is aware of them).

Write a self-appraisal using the appraisal form. Again, whether or not the organization requires self-appraisal as part of the performance evaluation process, it's a good idea for the individual to draft a self-appraisal before sitting down for the formal performance review.

Consider any revisions needed to your key position, responsibilities, goals, objectives, competencies, and development plans for the next performance review cycle. Creating an accomplishments list and writing a self-appraisal uncovers areas of the job that have changed since the original performance-planning meeting was held. Some projects have been finished; some goals have been achieved or abandoned. Some key job responsibilities have shifted in importance. The annual performance appraisal review is the ideal time to recognize job changes and discuss how the job will be different in the upcoming year.

Prepare for the performance review meeting. Each individual should ask herself: What do I want to get out of this performance review? What are the questions that I want to get the answers to? What are the accomplishments over the year that I want to make sure my boss recognizes? What do I need to do to be a prime candidate the next time a promotional opportunity comes around?

4.4 What are my boss's responsibilities in the performance assessment phase? Does she have to review and approve my appraisals before I deliver them to my staff?

In the performance assessment phase, the reviewer—the supervisor's supervisor—has a specific set of responsibilities. The primary ones are to:

- Ensure timely completion of performance reviews.
- Ensure fair, thorough, and complete reviews.
- Ensure inter-rater reliability.
- Ensure tough-minded, demanding performance standards are set.
- Coach appraisers for success.

Tell Me More

The reviewer is the individual who is responsible for reviewing performance appraisals written by his or her subordinate managers before they go over those appraisals with their employees. If you are a manager who not only has to write appraisals but also has to review those written by managers who report to you, here are the key responsibilities that you need to meet in your reviewer role:

Ensure timely completion of performance reviews. Your first responsibility is to make sure that all managers in your work unit complete their performance appraisals on time. Enough said.

Ensure fair, thorough, and complete reviews. While the people whose performance reviews you'll be reviewing don't work directly for you, you probably know all of them reasonably well. Do the appraisals that their managers have written conform with your feelings about how well they have done? Are all aspects of their performance covered? Does it appear that any personal biases—positive or negative—are creeping in? If so, discuss these with the appraisal writer.

Ensure inter-rater reliability. Are all of your managers applying the same standards to their people? Does one manager put more emphasis on competencies than another? Your job here is to make sure that an individual who performed at a certain level will get the same performance appraisal rating, whether the appraisal is written by manager A, manager B, or manager C.

Ensure tough-minded, demanding performance standards are set. Now your job gets harder. Are some of your managers more lenient or tougher than others? Unless there are compelling reasons to the contrary, the standards of the toughest appraiser in your work group should set the tone for all managers charged with doing performance appraisals.

Red Flag

It's very likely that different managers have different performance expectations and standards. Some are likely to be tough and demanding while others are pushover pussycats. It's an easy temptation for the reviewer to coax the more demanding managers to soften their standards ("Gee, Jim, you seem to be pretty hard on Harry"). It is more difficult to force reluctant raters into holding people's feet to the high-performance fire ("Diane, your people are putting forth any level of effort that they feel like and you're not holding them accountable"). It's more difficult to raise performance standards than it is to lower them, but—hey, pal—that's why you're the boss!

Coach appraisers for success. Once you have reviewed and approved the written performance appraisals your managers have written, be sure to review their plans for conducting the appraisal discussion. It's likely that some of your managers may never have delivered a performance appraisal before. Help them succeed by coaching them on your experience or engaging in a practice session.

4.5 Should I ask the individual whose performance appraisal I am preparing to make up a list of accomplishments?

Yes. Requesting a list of their accomplishments and achievements from each individual over the course of the year is one of the most effective ways to begin the performance assessment process.

Tell Me More

The best way to start the performance assessment phase of the process is for the manager to request an accomplishments list from each person she'll be evaluating. The manager might say something like this:

> Sam, over the next few weeks I'll be writing your annual performance appraisal. Before I even begin thinking about your appraisal, though, I'd like you to send me a list of all of the things you've done this year that you really feel good about . . . all of your achievements and accomplishments. It doesn't have to be formal—just send me an e-mail or write it on the back of an envelope.
>
> And by the way—if there's anything that you did over the past twelve months that didn't turn out as well as you would have liked, don't include that. I am not interested in getting a balanced summary. I only want to know about the things you've done this year that you are really proud of.

To begin, a request like this one puts a very appropriate and positive spin on the whole performance appraisal process. Too often people feel that the purpose of performance appraisal is to point out all of their faults, flaws, and failings over the course of the year (and the way some managers conduct performance appraisal discussions, it's no wonder people feel this way.) A request for an accomplishments list, particularly when the manager specifically asks the individual not to include anything that is not a genuine source of pride, convinces the people receiving the request that the manager genuinely wants to focus on people's strengths and successes in doing a performance review.

Here, though, is the more important reason for asking for an accomplishments list. For a manager, there are few things more embarrassing than giving Sally her performance review in early December, watching her read it, and hearing her wail, "But you didn't even mention the Thompson project I did last February!" You then realize that you had forgotten all about one of her most important contributions to the company in the entire twelve months. That's a managerial gaffe that will never be forgotten.

Asking for an accomplishments list removes the possibility of getting caught in that embarrassing trap. Now the manager will receive Sally's list of accomplishments, discover the forgotten Thompson project at the top of her list, and say to himself, "Oh, dear! I forgot all about it. It's a good thing I asked for this list." The manager may forget about some of the individual's accomplishments; the individual won't.

Hot Tip

Another reason for asking for the accomplishments list is that it will give you a good perspective on how the individual looks at her own performance. Is her accomplishments list reasonable, demonstrating a mature view of genuine achievements over the course of the year? Or is it filled with any possible positive actions, most so minor that they are hardly worth mentioning? Is the list remarkable for how short it is, and how trivial the accomplishments listed? Asking for the accomplishments list will give the supervisor a good heads-up for what he might expect in the appraisal discussion, particularly if his judgments about the value of the individual's accomplishments are not as stellar as she sees them to be.

4.6 Should I ask the individual to complete a self-appraisal using the company's performance appraisal form?

First, follow your company's policy. Many organizations request that all employees complete a self-appraisal as part of the organization's performance management system. If your company does have such a requirement, ask each individual to complete the self-appraisal as policy dictates.

If there is no requirement for self-appraisal, it's still a good idea. The hour that the person spends reflecting on just how well she performed in the last twelve months may be far more valuable than anything you say as the supervisor during the appraisal discussion.

Tell Me More

To begin, self-appraisal should always be a voluntary process. People should be invited/requested/permitted to complete a self-appraisal as part of the performance management process, but they should never be required/coerced/compelled to do so. Compelling self-appraisal will defeat the benefit of having people think carefully about how they have performed over the year. It will likely bring resentment ("That's your job, not mine!"). It may even provoke a refusal. What is the manager to do when the employee says, "I really don't feel comfortable with doing a self-appraisal . . . I would prefer not to?" Will the manager make the self-appraisal a condition of employment and insist that the individual complete the form on pain of termination? And what possible value will that self-appraisal have?

A better approach is simply to point out that self-appraisal has some benefits and ask informally that the individual complete one.

Another important issue involves the timing of the employee's delivery of her self-appraisal to the manager. Should the individual bring it to the performance appraisal review meeting so that she and the manager can look at what each other has written at the same time, or should the individual send the self-appraisal to the manager well in advance so that the manager can use the employee's self-appraisal as a data source for constructing the official appraisal?

Both approaches have benefits and disadvantages. The most important thing is clear communication with the individual about the purpose of the self-appraisal and the mechanics of delivering it. The manager can say, "Sam, as part of our process we ask every person to complete a self-appraisal of his own performance. Here's a blank copy of the form. I'd like you to complete it and send me a copy by next Thursday so I can take your insights into consideration as I'm writing the official appraisal." The manager could just as easily say, "Sam, we routinely ask every employee to write a self-appraisal as part of our performance management process. Here's a copy of the form for you to use. Give it some thought, write a self-appraisal, and bring it with you when we get together next week to review the official appraisal I'm writing."

Red Flag

Asking for an accomplishments list and requesting self-appraisals are appropriate only when the individual's performance is at least meeting the organization's standards. If the individual's performance is below standard, or if there is a specific performance issue that could jeopardize continued employment if it is not immediately corrected, avoid asking for a self-appraisal or an accomplishments list. The reason is that in the case of a marginal performer, it's important for the manager to have great control over the situation. Inviting a self-appraisal or an accomplishments list provokes discussion of the way the employee sees the situation and the way the manager sees it. With people whose performance is fully successful, that's appropriate. With a marginal performer, it's not. The manager needs to be in charge of the meeting and explain that there must be an immediate correction of the situation or significantly unhappy consequences will follow.

4.7 I have to write a performance appraisal. Where do I start?

Here is a four-step process for writing an effective performance appraisal:

1. Gather all of your information.
2. Get the big picture—the core message—clearly in mind, by asking:

   - "What is the single most important message I want to communicate about the individual's performance through this performance appraisal?"

3. Identify the three key elements:

- Particular strengths demonstrated
- Most critical needs for improvement
- Most important development needs

4. Muster your courage to tell the truth:

- Most accurate rating category for each individual objective
- Most accurate narrative description for each explanation or summary

Tell Me More

Gather all of your information. You'll need information about both the job itself and the way the person did the job. In the next few pages we'll tell you exactly what information you need to collect.

Get the big picture—the core message—clearly in mind. This is one of the most critical steps in writing a performance appraisal that brings about performance improvement.

The research on performance appraisal is consistent—and dismaying. Consistently, performance appraisal research demonstrates that people retain very little of what they are told in a performance appraisal discussion. What little they do remember, they usually misunderstand. That is the challenge managers face in trying to communicate clearly about performance in the course of an appraisal discussion.

To overcome this challenge, it's important to develop a clear core message. What is the core message? It is the single most important idea that you want to get across in the course of a performance appraisal discussion.

Here's how to think about it. Imagine that a few weeks ago you had your annual performance appraisal discussion with Joanne. This morning, as you're walking down the hall, you see her walking toward you. You pull her aside and say, "Joanne, a few weeks ago we had a performance appraisal discussion. Tell me something . . . what do you remember from that discussion?"

Joanne, caught off-guard and unprepared for your question, will hesitate and stammer a little bit. Then she's likely to say, "Well, one thing for sure that I remember that you said was . . ."

What do you want her to remember? What is that one thing that you want to have stuck in her memory? Whatever it is, that is your core message.

Before writing anything on the appraisal form, think about what it is that you want the individual to get out of the discussion. One problem with performance appraisal discussions is that the manager tries to communicate too much information. Instead of trying to communicate thirty different things, you'll be much more successful trying to communicate three genuinely important things.

If you have clearly identified one core message, it will then be easy to continually focus the discussion on that key item. You'll discuss plenty of different topics in the course of a performance appraisal meeting, but whenever you need to get back to the main point, it will be easy to say, "Well, Robert, that brings us back to the key point again," and then restate your core message one more time.

Identify the key elements. There are three key elements to any performance assessment: the particular strengths that the individual displayed; the most serious problem areas or improvement needs; and the most important development needs for the individual's future with the organization.

Muster your courage to tell the truth. This is by far the most important requirement for performance appraisal success. If the manager doesn't have the courage to tell the truth about the individual's performance, then the process will be a sham.

4.8 What information do I need to write a valid performance appraisal?

You'll need information about four different factors that contribute to an effective performance appraisal:

1. The job
2. The jobholder
3. The person
4. The self-appraisal or accomplishments list

Tell Me More

The Job. Begin by rereading the job description for the individual. That is your very first responsibility in getting ready to do a performance appraisal. You are not evaluating Charlie—you are evaluating how well Charlie did this particular job. Start therefore by getting the job clearly in mind.

It may be that Charlie's job description isn't very good. It's not completely accurate. It describes some things that he's really not responsible for and omits some critical responsibilities. Again, reading the job description helps you understand exactly what Charlie's job actually is, since you'll be able to compare his real day-to-day job with the somewhat artificial construct described in the official job description. (And this is an excellent time to get the wheels in motion to get the outmoded job description revised.)

Next, pull out your copy of the performance appraisal form with the notes that the individual took during the performance-planning meeting at the start of the year. Review the goals that you set and the discussion you had about the key job responsibilities. Again, your focus is on getting a clear understanding of exactly what the job you're assessing involves.

Finally, answer these questions:

- Why did the organization create this job?
- What are the most important ways in which a person doing this job should spend her time?
- What are the two or three most important duties of a person holding this job?
- If someone asked me what it takes to be successful in this job, what would I say?
- What is the easiest way to tell whether this job is being done well?

The answers to these questions will give you a solid fix on exactly what the job itself is. And before you can assess how well someone did a job, you must know what the job actually is.

The Jobholder. Now is the time to start collecting all of the available information about the person doing the job. The most valuable source of information is all of the notes and entries you made in your performance log. (If you haven't been keeping a performance log or diary for each of the people you're responsible for supervising, you'll appreciate the value of it now.)

Some of the information will be numerical and quantitative. Some of it will be descriptive and qualitative. Get it all together.

Next, review both your notes and your memory for critical incidents. Critical incidents are events where the individual demonstrated either particularly good or poor performance.

What have you observed in the person's performance that was worth remembering for the appraisal discussion? Behavioral observations are another source of data.

The Person. Now it's time to consider Charlie himself. How does his performance this year compare with how he's performed in previous years? Is he staying steady (in the face of rising performance expectations), gradually improving, greatly improving, or falling behind? How does his performance compare with the performance of people doing similar jobs? What action has he taken on items that you identified as needing attention during the midterm review? Did he get right to work on your suggestions or did he ignore the recommendations you made? How effective have his efforts been?

The Self-Appraisal and Accomplishments List. If you asked the individual to prepare a list of accomplishments or complete a self-appraisal (and return it to you in advance), this will be a worthwhile source of performance data. Has the person identified all of her important accomplishments—the ones that you are personally familiar with? Are there significant differences between your opinion of the quality of the individual's work and her own?

Is there any evidence of "gilding the lily"—presenting minor attainments as colossal triumphs?

Finally, is the individual unduly harsh or lenient in the evaluation of her own performance?

Gathering data from these four sources—the job, the jobholder, the person, and the accomplishments list—will give you a complete perspective on the individual's job performance.

4.9 What about collecting data from other people to use on the performance appraisal form? Would it be a good idea to ask for information from a salesman's customers, or ask a manager's subordinates about her performance as a supervisor?

Other people may have far more information than the manager himself may have. Customers know more about a salesman's customer relations performance than the sales manager knows; subordinates know more about their boss's supervisory abilities than the boss's boss can hope to know.

But there are some ethical responsibilities involved here. Before calling a group of a salesman's customers to ask them about the quality of service he provides, or surveying a work team about how good a job their supervisor does in motivating and recognizing them, it's appropriate to get the individual involved in—or at least aware of—this data-collection effort.

Tell Me More

The best time to consider this is during the performance-planning discussion at the start of the year. In the discussions with the salesman and supervisor, the manager and the individual will agree that customer relations and supervisory skills will be two aspects of performance that are important to assess. It is logical for the manager to ask the individual. "Jack, how will I get the information I need to assess your performance in the customer relations area?" Or, "Marie, what do you think is the best way for me to find out about your supervisory skills?"

In each case, of course, the answer is obvious: Talk with my customers/subordinates.

The manager is then able to ask, "How do you suggest that I do this?" The best approach for the customer data would probably be to ask them to fill out some simple survey. For the subordinates, a written survey would work, as might a couple of interviews or an invitation to submit a confidential narrative about the way the supervisor works with those on the team.

In both cases, make the individual responsible for gathering the data. The salesman should be the person to draft the customer service survey and, after the manager reviews and approves it, distribute it to a representative sample of his customers. The supervisor can discuss the need to get the manager the information needed for the supervisor's performance appraisal during a staff meeting.

Hot Tip

The key point is this: Make the individual responsible for collecting the data about his own performance.

4.10   I've asked the employee to write a self-appraisal. Should I use what the employee has written in the self-appraisal as part of the official appraisal I'm writing?

Only if what the employee has written exactly reflects your own view of the quality of her performance.

Some individuals have discovered that when they are called upon to write a self-appraisal, the boss is actually attempting to delegate the entire performance appraisal chore to the subordinate. In this case, the shrewd subordinate should write a glowing review of herself with all strengths praised and all flaws minimized, particularly if the appraisal rating will connect with compensation decisions or promotability.

The wise manager uses the subordinate's self-appraisal as only one nugget in a whole mine of performance information. However, if the employee has described her performance in a way that is particularly accurate and well written, there is no reason not to copy the employee's words into the official appraisal.

4.11 Should I put more emphasis on the results the individual achieved or on the way the person went about doing the job?

Put more emphasis on the results. Ultimately, getting the job done is more important than the way in which the results were brought about (assuming legal and ethical means were used).

Tell Me More

Some organizations provide for various objectives to be weighted, or allocate a certain number of points between the competencies portion of the performance appraisal instrument and the part that evaluates the individual's performance against goals, objectives, and key job responsibilities. If your organization provides for a specific weighting scheme, follow the procedures provided.

Most organizations, however, don't provide predetermined weightings. Managers have discretion about the amount of emphasis to place on different aspects of performance. If this is the case in your company, take advantage of the flexibility you've been provided. In your performance-planning discussion, let the individual know which portions of the performance appraisal form you're going to put the greatest emphasis on. If you feel that Harry should pay particular attention to his performance in one particular competency area, tell him at the start of the year that that competency is going to count more than any of the others.

It's not a good idea to try to assign specific percentages or to allocate one hundred points to various parts of the form. While this approach might seem logical, it ends up forcing managers and employees to make trivial distinctions. Worse, it leads to making the determination of an employee's final rating into an arithmetic problem.

A better approach is simply to indicate high, medium, and low when you are talking about the relative importance of various elements to be assessed.

4.12   One of my subordinates works in a different city and I don't see her very much. How can I appraise her performance accurately?

This is an easy one. The mistake appraisers make in this case is to assume that it's their job to figure out an answer to the question. It's not. Make it the subordinate's job.

Tell Me More

You're in headquarters in Cincinnati; Mary runs the regional office in Des Moines. The only time you get to see her is on her quarterly corporate visits and your occasional travels to Iowa. But still you have to appraise her performance.

It's no different if the subordinate is in a different building, or even just a different office. Managers are frequently placed in the position of having to accurately assess the performance of someone whom they don't see very often. How do you do this fairly?

Get together with Mary at the start of the appraisal cycle. Explain the dilemma: "Mary, one of the challenges we face is that I'm responsible for doing your performance appraisal and yet we don't have much contact with each other. I need you to come up with a plan that will allow me to get all of the information I need to do an honest job of evaluating your performance. Over the next couple of weeks, I'd like you to figure out how I will be able to get a complete picture of the contributions you're making." The quality of Mary's plan then becomes another factor to consider in assessing her performance.

Hot Tip

When difficult performance-related challenges arise, too often managers feel that they have to figure everything out themselves. This forces an inappropriate burden on the manager. A more effective approach is to place the responsibility for finding a solution on the person who is the most concerned with it: the subordinate. For example, one of Amanda's key responsibilities involves being gracious to particularly rude and nasty customers. But because she is so skilled at this (she tells you) you don't appreciate how good a job she does because they're all smiles when they arrive at your desk. Instead of trying to figure out how you'll get the information you need on her performance, make her responsible for generating it. Say: "Amanda, you're right. It is important for me to know how well you're doing in taking care of our customers who are upset, and I don't see very many upset customers. Why don't you think about it and come up with a plan for how I can get the information I need in order to assess your customer handling skills?" Then wait to see the plan Amanda develops.

4.13 Should I include the employee's successes and failures in completing the development plan as part of his formal performance appraisal?

No. Development is development—it's not job performance. Giving someone a high performance appraisal rating because that person completed an important and challenging development plan (while missing several important performance expectations) is as unfair as gigging someone whose performance made the whole department shine because he sacrificed his development plan to turn in that outstanding performance.

Keep performance and development separate.

4.14 What are "rating errors"?

Rating errors are mistakes in judgment that result from allowing extraneous factors to influence our decisions about the quality of someone's job performance. For example, consider the guilt-by-association error: The employees that Samantha hangs around with are poor performers and have bad work habits. As a result, her boss rates Samantha's performance low without taking into account the fact that, in spite of her poor taste in friends, the quality of her work is actually quite high. That's a rating error.

Tell Me More

Besides the unusual rating error of guilt by association, there are ten more common rating errors that show up when managers complete performance appraisal on their subordinates. Figure 4-1 provides a definition of each of these rating errors and an example of how it might show up in a performance appraisal.

To avoid rating errors, review the examples in Figure 4-1 every time you complete a performance appraisal. If you have committed a rating error, probably just reviewing the list will be sufficient to make the error stand out.

4.15   Should I go over the employee's appraisal with my manager before I review it with the individual?

Yes. Reviewing your performance appraisal of a subordinate before you hold the appraisal review discussion with that person is a very wise thing to do.

Tell Me More

Here are the benefits of reviewing your performance appraisals of your staff with your boss before you discuss them with the members of the team:

Error Reduction. Your boss might just spot some mistakes you have made in writing the performance appraisals. Some of the mistakes might be minor, but having another person review the appraisal before it's delivered may also prevent some hugely embarrassing blunders. (Your boss might just say, "Correct me if I'm wrong, but wasn't it Harriet who told our best customer to go piss up a rope last winter, not Molly?" It would be good to correct that mistake before you give Molly the appraisal with the inaccurate accusation on it.)

Broader Organizational Scope. Your boss is probably reasonably familiar with the quality of work done by the people under your direct supervision. She's also familiar with the quality of work done by people who work for other supervisors. It may well be that where you have rated a person as fully successful, your boss can suggest that based on the performance of others and the ratings they have been given, a rating

(text continues on page 96)

Figure 4-1. Common rating errors.

Error	Definition	Example
Attractiveness effect	The well-documented tendencies for people to assume that people who are physically attractive are also superior performers.	Ronald, a customer service supervisor, rated those subordinates who were tall, slender, and good-looking higher than she rated those who were just average in appearance, even though there was no significant difference in the quality of their work.
Attribution bias	The tendency to attribute performance failings to factors under the control of the individual and performance successes to external causes.	Harriet, a manager with a mixture of both excellent and mediocre performers in her work group, attributes the successes of the former group to the quality of her leadership and the failings of the latter group to their bad attitudes and inherent laziness.
Central tendency	The inclination to rate people in the middle of the scale even when their performance clearly warrants a substantially higher or lower rating.	Out of an erroneous belief that the law required companies to treat all employees the same, and a conscious desire to avoid confrontation, Harold rated all seven of the employees in his work group as fully successful despite significant differences in their performance.
First impression error	The tendency of a manager to make an initial positive or negative judgment of an employee and allow that first impression to color or distort later information.	Rachel, a manager new to a work group, noticed one employee, who was going through a divorce, performing poorly. Within a month the employee's performance had returned to its previous high level, but Rachel's opinion of the individual's performance was adversely affected by the initial negative impression.

(continues)

Figure 4-1. (Continued).

Error	Definition	Example
Halo/horns effect	Inappropriate generalizations from one aspect of an individual's performance to all areas of that person's performance.	Jeff was outstanding in his ability to get delinquent customers to pay up. His excellence in this important area caused his manager to unthinkingly rate him highly in unrelated areas where his performance was actually mediocre.
High potential error	Confusing an individual's future potential with his current performance.	Luis has a graduate degree from a prestigious university and was selected for the company's fasttrack training program. As a result, his manager rated his performance as superior when actually it was mediocre.
Negative and positive skew	The opposite of central tendency. The rating of all individuals as higher or lower than their performance actually warrants.	Susan rates all of her employees higher than she feels they actually deserve, in the misguided hope that this will cause them to live up to the high rating they have been given. Carlos sets impossibly high standards and expectations and is proud of never having met a subordinate who deserved a superior rating.
Past performance error	Permitting an individual's poor (or excellent) performance in a previous rating period to color the manager's judgment about her performance in this rating period.	Last year Alicia was a distinguished performer and received the highest appraisal rating. This year her manager again rated her distinguished, even though her performance this year was no better than other employees who were rated fully successful.

Recency effect	The tendency for minor events that have happened recently to have more influence on the rating than major events of many months ago.	Victoria kept no formal records of the overall performance or critical incidents of her work group of twelve people during the course of the year. When she began writing their appraisals, she discovered that the only examples she could provide for either positive or negative performance had happened in the last two months.
Similar-to-me effect	The tendency of individuals to rate people who resemble themselves higher than they rate others.	Carol, a single mother of four small children, had prevailed in her efforts to succeed and had been promoted to manager. She unwittingly rated several women who were also single mothers higher than their performance warranted.
Stereotyping	The tendency to generalize across groups and ignore individual differences.	Waldo is quiet and reserved, almost meek—about as far from the conventional cliché of a salesman as can be imagined. His sales record, however, is one of the best in the company. But his boss rated his performance lower than that of other salespeople since he didn't fit the mold, ignoring the results that Waldo had produced.

Source: Grote Consulting Corporation.

of "superior" (or perhaps, "needs improvement") might be more appropriate.

Less Chance of Personality Factors or Rating Errors Playing an Inappropriate Part in the Appraisal. If a supervisor has to defend a negative performance appraisal of a subordinate to his boss before he can deliver the bad news to the individual, there's less chance that a personal grudge or a rating error will mar the accuracy of the evaluation. It's easy for an employee to complain that the reason he got a bad performance review was that the boss didn't like him. It's more difficult for that person to claim that the bad review was a function of a conspiracy between the boss and his boss, both sharing the secret objective of sticking it to an innocent subordinate.

Less Likelihood of Challenge. If the employee with a poor performance rating sees the signatures of both his immediate supervisor and that person's superior, he's less likely to challenge the bad rating as merely a manifestation of a personality clash or some other inappropriate cause, since at least two people share a common view of the low quality of his performance.

Greater Defensibility. If the employee does challenge a performance appraisal rating, there's less chance that the challenge will be sustained if the organization can demonstrate that the supervisor's appraisal rating was reviewed and approved in advance by a more senior member of management.

Chance to Practice. Reviewing your performance appraisal ratings with your boss in advance, particularly those that have a high probability of generating an adversarial reaction, may give you the chance to plan your response if the employee acts in a defensive and challenging manner. It gives you the opportunity to say, "I think Marty may respond very negatively to this review, boss. Let me tell you about what I think she may say and how I'm planning to respond. I'd like to get any suggestions that you have."

Hot Tip

If your boss recommends any changes in the narrative you have written or the ratings you have decided on, you will have more insight into your boss's way of thinking in an important area. That is always valuable.

4.16   How do I go about convincing my boss (assuming her approval is needed) that one of my people deserves a particularly positive or negative review?

Begin laying the groundwork well in advance of the time when you actually show your boss the completed appraisal you have written on the individual and ask her to approve it.

Tell Me More

There's an old piece of advice that recommends getting "all your ducks in a line" before taking action. That's good advice in this situation.

When you first start thinking about Herman's performance in preparation for the appraisal you're going to have to write, and you realize that his performance is well outside the fully successful area (either in a positive or negative direction), you're going to have to prepare your boss for an exceptional performance review.

Let's assume that Herman's performance has been less than adequate. You've had a couple of informal conversations with him about the need to improve, but you haven't said anything to your boss since you had hoped the issue could be resolved without having to bring it to the attention of higher management.

But your efforts to get Herman to change haven't succeeded. In spite of your conversations with him, his performance is still marginal and performance appraisal time is rolling around. You need to prepare your boss for what will be a significantly bad performance appraisal that she will have to approve.

You might mention in the course of a routine conversation with your boss that you're about to start work on writing the performance appraisals for people in your department and that one of them—Herman's—doesn't look like it's going to be too good. If your boss asks you questions about why you feel that way, bring up some of the information that justifies the low appraisal rating. Tell your boss about the conversations you have had with Herman and the lack of results.

Your boss may feel that rating anyone's performance at the low end of the rating scale is a negative reflection on her managerial skills and may be resistant to approving a less-than-satisfactory rating. In this case you'll need to have all your supporting documents ready when the time comes. It may be that your boss is concerned about the fairness of someone's getting a black mark on a performance appraisal that will permanently reside in his personnel file. In this case you'll need to point out the unfairness to good performers of giving a satisfactory rating to someone who hasn't earned it.

It may also be that your boss is reluctant to approve a particularly high performance appraisal rating. The cause may be that the boss doesn't want to highlight the performance of a star and increase the possibility of that person's being promoted out of the unit. It may be that the boss is hesitant because high ratings produce high merit increases and she doesn't want the salary budget to get out of kilter.

Whatever the reason, you have a sales job to do. Lay the groundwork well in advance of the time your boss reads the review and has to sign it. Just as the standard advice recommends that the individual get no surprises in the course of a performance appraisal discussion (more on that later), so your boss should never get any surprises when she's asked to approve an appraisal you have written.

4.17   If the appraiser's boss approves the appraisal before the employee sees it, hasn't the door been closed on the possibility of any changes?

It's true: Once an appraiser has written a performance appraisal and has achieved his boss's blessing, the appraiser is unlikely to be willing to change the appraisal, even if the employee is able to present solid evidence and persuasive arguments about why the appraisal narrative and rating, even though approved, is inaccurate.

Employees may also be reluctant to expend much energy discussing an appraisal with which they disagree, since it has already been seen and signed off on by the boss, the boss's boss, other bosses, and personnel too. "You can't fight City Hall," they say to themselves. "It's better to grin and bear it."

Tell Me More

The alternative is to have the appraising manager carry out the entire performance appraisal procedure, including writing the narrative and discussing it with the subordinate before submitting it to his boss and personnel for review and filing. This approach will probably only work in organizations where the performance appraisal grade is only one factor in making the compensation change decision, where a high degree of trust exists throughout the organization, and where supervisors, managers, and human resources specialists at all levels are sophisticated and experienced.

The benefits of this approach include empowering lower level managers to act in a highly sensitive area of the organization's operation, increasing the probability that the ultimate appraisal document will reflect a genuine understanding (if not complete agreement) between rater and ratee, and a far greater likelihood of open discussions about performance and the areas where change and development are needed. The risks, however, are real: If an upper manager disagrees with the appraisal that a junior has assigned to a subordinate's performance, that junior manager will be in the uncomfortable position of having to go back to the employee and confess that he couldn't get the appraisal past his boss. Conversely, upper-level managers may be reluctant to recommend obvious and necessary changes in the form since it has already been reviewed with the individual.

4.18 The individual failed to achieve an important objective, but there were extenuating circumstances. How should I rate her performance?

This is a situation where the narrative section of the appraisal form is critical. As a rater, you have an ethical responsibility to tell the truth. If the objective wasn't met, say so.

But you also have a responsibility to tell the whole story. If the failure to meet the objective was completely outside the individual's control (e.g., the client she was assigned to work with declared bankruptcy in the middle of the project), focus on two areas: First, evaluate the quality of her performance independent of the results. Second, focus on the damage-control efforts she put forth to minimize the impact of the failure. In other words, did she pick up any signs that the project or the client was in trouble, or was she blindsided by the bad news? Did she immediately get to work to minimize the damage or did she just helplessly watch the chips fall? If the project had continued, would the work that she did have been a smashing success?

If your performance appraisal form provides the option of indicating "unable to rate," this is a time when that block can appropriately be checked.

4.19   In writing the individual's performance appraisal, should I consider how well he performs compared with other people in the department who are doing the same job?

Yes.

There are only three bases of comparison that you have available in assessing the quality of someone's performance: Comparison with others, predetermined standards, and gut feeling.

Tell Me More

Comparison with Others. How well did this person perform compared with other people doing the same job? Did she do better or worse than her predecessor? These are the questions you ask in assessing performance based on comparison with others.

Some people argue that it isn't fair to compare people against each other; that there should be independent standards. Although it is certainly beneficial to have independent standards, comparing the performance of one individual with that of another helps the manager assess whether his standards are reasonable, too lenient, or too tough.

Predetermined Standards. This is the ideal way for performance expectations to be set. At the beginning of the year, the boss and subordinate agree that fully successful performance will involve selling 254 units per quarter, reducing sales expense by 17 percent, and increasing the average customer satisfaction score by 12 points.

Although predetermined standards are ideal, they frequently are difficult to determine. The more complex the job, the more difficult it is going to be to come up with precise predetermined standards of performance.

The expectation for a recruiter might be that she significantly increase the overall quality of new employees recruited for the management-training program. That's an important goal, but where is the quantifiable standard to assess how well she has done? Although some indicators may be available (e.g., an increase in the number of candidates from top-tier schools, a reduction in the number of wash-outs), these don't directly measure the quality of the new hires. The more that job success is a function of the quality of the individual's performance, the less likely that the manager is going to find valid predetermined standards of performance.

Gut Feeling. Gut feeling as a basis for assessing performance tends to be ridiculed as completely inappropriate. It's not.

In addition to being able to measure outcomes with quantifiable, countable measures and predetermined standards, the intuitive skills of a manager are critically important. Consider this sentence from an actual performance appraisal written by a United States Army major about the performance of a captain: "CPT Lee has an intuitive feel for combat operations and her innate leadership skills allow her to consistently make the correct decisions while under pressure."

In a situation involving a hostile enemy maneuver, peoples' lives depend on their leaders' "intuitive feel for combat operations" and their "innate leadership skills." There is no quantitative measure or predetermined standard available to assess these critically important abilities. But to prevent an assessor from using his experience, judgment, perception, and gut feeling because countable units of performance are absent, would be foolishness itself.

4.20 Our performance appraisal form has a rating scale that asks whether the performance failed to meet expectations/met some expectations/met all expectations/exceeded expectations/far exceeded expectations. If I haven't discussed my expectations with the employee, how do I rate performance?

Contained in this question is the best argument for conducting a performance-planning discussion at the beginning of the year. If you don't know what you're looking for, how will you know when you find it? Ideally the manager and the individual will discuss each of the manager's expectations at the start of the year and will come to an understanding of what the manager considers to be fully successful performance. If they do this, it will not only make it easier for the manager to accurately assess the quality of the job the individual has done, it will also increase the probability that then two of them will agree on the accuracy of the assessment. But if no expectations have been set, then it's more difficult for the manager and more likely that the two parties won't see eye to eye.

But often the performance-planning discussion hasn't taken place or, more likely, over the course of the year new programs, expectations, and objectives have arisen that weren't subject to formal determination and communication of objectives. In this case, the manager must simply assess the quality of performance using his experience with similar people facing similar assignments. The manager needs to be prepared, too, if the assessment is anything other than stellar, to discuss the employee's reasonable rejoinder: "Why didn't you tell me what you wanted at the beginning of the year?"

Tell Me More

An effective way to justify and explain the ratings you are assigning to the individual's performance is to correlate the rating of the performance with the message that you are trying to send the individual about the quality of his performance. For example, with the rating scheme of far exceeded expectations/exceeded expectations/achieved expectations/met some expectations/did not meet expectations, the message sent by each rating category is as follows:

Far Exceeded Expectations. Your performance has been genuinely outstanding. Few other people have ever produced the results that you have achieved. You far exceed all reasonable performance expectations. Other people talk about the high quality of your work. You have achieved remarkable success in both producing highly impressive results and in developing uncommonly successful working relationships. The quality of your work is so outstanding that no rating other than "far exceeded expectations" could even be considered. No one would dispute that you are one of the most talented individuals in our organization. Performance at your level of quality is truly rare.

Exceeded Expectations. Your job performance is significantly and noticeably better than that of other people. There are no areas in which you are not entirely proficient. The high quality of your work provides a model to others in the organization, both in terms of the results you achieve and in your interactions with others to achieve those results. There is no area in which your work needs to be improved. You routinely exceed expectations. The quality of performance you provide is an example for other people to aim for. You are a great asset to this organization.

Met All Expectations. You are doing a completely satisfactory and fully respectable job. Your performance in every area of your job is entirely competent, efficient, and constructive. There are several areas in which your job performance is better than average and no part where specific improvement is needed. Both the results you achieve and the way in which you go about performing your job are good examples to others. You are very well qualified for this position. You fully meet all job expectations and frequently exceed them. You can be proud of the quality of your work.

Met Some Expectations. While you do some parts of your job fairly well, there are other parts that you do not perform at a fully acceptable level. You are doing reasonably well, particularly if you haven't been doing this job for a lengthy period, but you're not yet at a totally competent level of performance. You often are able to act independently, but your work requires more supervision than should be necessary. Your performance in many ways is good, but it needs to be better.

Failed to Meet Expectations. Your performance in not acceptable. It does not meet the minimum expectations for this job. You must make an immediate and dramatic correction.

Hot Tip

Notice that the narrative for the middle rating had no suggestion that the performance was merely average, or just acceptable, or mediocre. Instead, the middle rating was written to communicate that the person's job performance was fully successful.

4.21 Our rating scale is numerical: one, two, three, four, and five, with five being the highest on the scale. Sally basically did a good job this year. Should I rate her a three, a four, or a five?

To begin, recognize that you've got a bad form. Good performance appraisal forms don't require appraisers to reduce people's performances to a number. But however the form is structured, you're stuck with it. Do your best.

Your best involves telling the truth. If Sally did a good job this year, and a good job is what you expect, then she met your expectations. Give her a rating of three.

4.22   Should employees in new roles be measured and evaluated the same as employees who have been in a role for a length of time?

Yes.

Tell Me More

It's likely that the person who is new to the job is not going to do it as well as someone with a couple of years of experience. That's understandable. But the manager will make a mistake if she tries to compensate for that individual's lack of experience by giving him an inflated rating.

It's an easy temptation to rationalize less-than-satisfactory performance by accommodating the individual's lack of experience. But rating an individual higher than she deserves because she is new on the job (even if the manager is sure the employee will earn the higher rating once she gains the necessary experience), is almost always a mistake.

First, the individual is probably aware that her performance isn't yet up to the fully satisfactory level. If the manager rates it as fully successful, then the message to the individual is that she is working for a manager with low standards. Even if the manager tries to justify the satisfactory appraisal rating by explaining that he is sure that her performance will improve to that level once she has some more experience, the individual realizes that she is working for a boss who is probably willing to cut corners and make excuses in other areas too.

A worse outcome will result if the individual takes the manager at his word and accepts the manager's judgment that her performance, poor as it is through lack of experience, is in fact fully satisfactory to the manager. By rating the performance at a higher level than deserved, the manager is providing a disincentive for the individual to improve.

Hot Tip

Most performance appraisal forms provide for both a rating and a narrative. The narrative is the area where the new-to-the-job explanation belongs. It is quite possible for the manager to write, "In spite of the fact that Sally has been on the job for four months, she is performing at a level that most people don't reach until they have twice the experience. While her specific performance rating reflects the fact that she has not yet achieved full mastery of the position, her efforts and successes to date suggest that she will soon be at a fully successful level of performance."

4.23   How can we take the "personal" out of a review and still give an accurate picture of the employee? For example, Joe's going through a divorce. His performance has suffered, but I empathize and want to give him a passing review.

It's understandable to want to avoid giving someone a mediocre review when we know that there are external factors that have caused a temporary performance deterioration. But the quality of the performance itself is what is being assessed. To fudge the facts and give someone a break because of external factors destroys the fundamental assumptions that performance appraisals are accurate and are written with integrity.

Tell Me More

There's a better way to handle a situation like this. Instead of writing a performance appraisal that in fact is not true, alert the individual that you have noticed a performance deterioration as soon as it becomes apparent. Talk with Joe about the fact that you're particularly concerned about his performance, not only because the quality of his work is suffering, but also because at performance appraisal time you won't be able to give him the satisfactory rating his good performance has earned him in the past.

There are two reasons for bringing up the possibility of a poor rating well before performance appraisal time. First, doing so can provide a significant incentive to change. Knowing that the boss has noticed the performance deterioration and will not make excuses when it's time to write the appraisal may have the beneficial effect of snapping Joe out of his slump and getting back to being the high performer that he was before.

Second, it alerts Joe to the consequence of continued poor performance so that there will be no surprises when the "fair" rating shows up where a "superior" rating had always been.

Red Flag

Making excuses for performance deficiencies is always a mistake. It is no more appropriate to write an inaccurate review to mask someone's failure to perform (even if for an understandable reason) than it would be to write an inaccurately negative review for someone who has performed at an excellent level because the manager feels that the excellent performance resulted from some temporary condition that is not likely to be sustained. Tell the truth and let the chips fall where they may.

4.24   One of my subordinates does a very good job . . . not breathtakingly outstanding, but solid and strong and better than average. Should I rate her in our middle category of fully successful or push her evaluation over the line and into the superior category? How do I figure out the right category?

Think about the individual's résumé. Ask yourself these questions:

- What results did the individual achieve in the last twelve months that were so significant that she needed to update her résumé to include them?
- What skills did the person acquire in the past year that were so important that he needed to update his résumé to include them?
- What individuals (internal and external) has this person so influenced that they need to be listed as references on the résumé?

Tell Me More

If your answer to the first question is, "Well, gee . . . Sally did a good job on all of the projects she was assigned and did a fine job with all of the things listed in her job description, but there wasn't anything that would cause her to rewrite her résumé," then the most accurate rating for her performance is the middle one.

If your answer to the second question is, "Well, Sally did go to a couple of training programs and learned how to input data into our control system, but that's not anything she would put on her résumé," then again the middle category is where her performance rating belongs.

Finally, if your answer to the last question is, "Well, Sally gets along just fine with everybody, but . . . ," then the right answer is to rate her as fully successful.

Thinking about the individual's résumé will help you make a good judgment about the most appropriate rating category to describe the person's performance. A highly effective operational test of superior performance is that the person would rewrite his or her résumé to reflect such quality of performance. If the quality of performance isn't such that the résumé needs to be rewritten, then it isn't high enough to earn a higher-than-middle rating.

Hot Tip

One additional benefit of using the "résumé test" in determining the final rating to be assigned to the individual's performance is that it makes explaining the rationale for the decision easier.

4.25   I have a concern about one of my people's performance, but I haven't previously discussed it with him. Is it okay to bring it up for the first time on the performance appraisal?

The traditional rule is well known and is always explained to managers when they go through performance appraisal training programs: No surprises in the performance appraisal discussion.

That is generally good advice. But what should a manager do when—as so often happens—the requirement that a performance appraisal be prepared causes the manager to critically review that performance and realize, for the first time, that the performance is definitely in need of significant improvement? Frequently, the first time that the manager consciously realizes that there is a significant concern with the employee's performance occurs when the manager must formally assess it.

Now the manager's in a pickle. On one hand, the conventional wisdom says: No surprises. Any concerns about the quality and quantity of a person's work should be discussed with that person during the course of the year and not delayed until appraisal time. It's inappropriate—cruel—to blindside the individual by describing hitherto undisclosed problems on the appraisal form since the individual has no chance to correct those problems before they become matters of record.

On the other hand, it may be that the first time the manager is aware that there is a serious concern with Tom's behavior and output occurs when she picks up the appraisal form and starts to write her assessment of Tom's contribution. "I would have told him before this if I had been aware of it, but I only became aware of it when I started completing the appraisal form. Now what do I do?"

Tell Me More

It's easy to duck the issue by condemning the manager for not having been more sensitive to the deteriorating quality of Tom's performance before the time for formal appraisal arrived. But that's a cheap shot. One of the benefits of a formal performance appraisal program is that it forces managers, on at least an annual basis, to review how well each subordinate is doing and talk to the person about that assessment. Yes, of course it would be nice if these conversations happened well before appraisal time, and everyone had all the time required to improve their performance so that they could get stellar ratings on the form. But that is unrealistic.

The right answer is to go right ahead and record the unpleasant facts on the form, knowing that Tom will be dismayed and will complain about having these issues brought up to him too late to do anything about it. The manager in this situation should simply admit that Tom's complaint is valid: She wishes she had been more aware of it earlier.

However, the fact that it would have been better to have discussed Tom's problems earlier doesn't take away the fact that those problems exist and are being brought to Tom's attention as soon as they came to the manager's notice. While it's unfortunate that at the time they were noticed, the appraisal was being prepared, the alternative—giving Tom an inaccurate inflated review while telling him on the Q.T. that the review as written is a lie—is even worse. In the first case, the manager's worst sin is being inattentive. In the latter, the manager admits to deceit.

It's an easy temptation to rationalize giving the individual an inappropriately high rating with the hope that the discussion of the actual unacceptable performance will cause the individual's efforts to rise to the level that was described in the form. This is unlikely. Instead, acknowledge that, while it would have been preferable to have discovered Tom's deficiencies and brought them to his attention earlier, the manager is still doing exactly what she is being paid to do—to bring any performance concern to the individual's attention as soon as it is discovered. That the time of discovery coincided with the time of performance appraisal doesn't detract a whit from the fact that the manager is doing the right thing.

Chapter 5

Performance Review

5.1   What is "performance review"?

Performance review is the final phase of an effective performance management system. It involves the individual and the manager discussing the performance appraisal document that the manager has created.

The performance management process both ends and begins anew with the performance review meeting. At the beginning of the meeting, the individual's past year's performance is reviewed and the success of the development plan is evaluated. At the end of the meeting, the appraiser and the individual set a date to create the plan for next year's goals, objectives, and development.

5.2   What are the manager's responsibilities in the performance review phase of the process?

The manager has seven primary responsibilities:

1. Review the agenda and time frame for meeting.
2. Review and discuss the performance appraisal you wrote and the individual's achievements list.
3. Listen and respond appropriately to the individual's perceptions and feedback.
4. Discuss your assessment of the individual's performance against objectives over the entire cycle, especially:

   - Strengths/achievements
   - Weaknesses/deficiencies
   - Development needs

5. Ensure full understanding of your core message.
6. Conclude the performance review discussion by scheduling the performance-planning meeting to plan next year's performance.
7. Handle all administrative requirements.

Tell Me More

Review the agenda and time frame for the meeting. Performance appraisal meetings always have some elements of awkwardness, no matter how well integrated the process is into the organization and how well the individual has performed. One easy way to put the person at ease and get the meeting off to a smooth start is by covering the logistical details first.

Review and discuss the performance appraisal you wrote and the individual's achievements list. This is the heart of the meeting. The manager and the individual review the performance appraisal the manager has written (and the self-appraisal if the individual has completed one).

Listen and respond appropriately to the individual's perceptions and feedback. The conversation needs to be a dialogue, not a monologue. The manager needs to explain how she came to the various judgments and assessments that she made in the writing of the appraisal and then listen to the individual's reactions and comments. The objective is to have both people end the meeting with a common understanding of the individual's performance. That can only happen if the manager genuinely listens to the individual's responses.

Discuss your assessment of the individual's performance against objectives over the entire cycle. There are three main areas that the discussion will focus on. First and most important are the strengths that the individual displayed during the course of the year. Your second focus is the areas where performance needs to be improved. Finally, assess the areas the individual should concentrate on for future growth and promotability.

Ensure full understanding of your core message. In Chapter 4, I recommended that managers always begin writing a performance appraisal by determining the core message that they want to communicate during the appraisal discussion. During the performance review, the manager needs to make sure that the individual understands the core message that the manager is sending.

Conclude the performance review discussion by scheduling the performance-planning meeting to plan next year's performance. The primary purpose of the performance review phase is to discuss the individual's performance over the appraisal period. Once the manager and individual have had a full discussion, it's appropriate to set a time to get back together to talk about the performance expectations, goals, and development plans for the next twelve months.

Handle all administrative requirements. Almost all performance appraisal procedures call for the individual to sign a copy of the form. Most allow the individual to write comments about her reaction to the review. A few appraisal procedures provide for an appeal process. And there may be other administrative issues. A comfortable way to wrap up the discussion is to go over the administrative requirements to make sure that all have been met.

5.3   What are the employee's responsibilities in the performance review phase?

Just as the manager has responsibilities, so too does the individual. There are six primary ones:

1. Discuss the achievements list you wrote.
2. Discuss what you achieved against your development plan.
3. Compare your assessment of your own performance with that of your appraiser.
4. Seek clarification for any assessments or examples that are unclear.
5. Consider how the appraiser's feedback will influence your performance plan for the upcoming appraisal period.
6. Listen and respond appropriately to the appraiser's perceptions and feedback.

Tell Me More

Discuss the achievements list you wrote. Wise managers ask each of their subordinates to create an accomplishments list to begin the performance assessment phase. This list is intended to provide the manager with a record of those achievements and accomplishments that the individual felt were the most important during the appraisal period. In the meeting, the individual should review the accomplishments list he prepared to make sure that the appraiser has appropriately incorporated his achievements during the review period.

Discuss what you achieved against your development plan. The individual is responsible for creating and executing the development plan. The performance review discussion is the ideal time to talk about what was accomplished and where the focus of development efforts needs to be in the upcoming year.

Compare your assessment of your own performance with that of your appraiser. Most of the time the individual and the manager come to essentially the same conclusions about the quality of the individual's performance—even when the performance hasn't been all that good. But it is important that the two participants talk through all areas of the appraisal, even areas where both the appraiser and the individual agree that the performance was excellent. And in those cases where there is a significant difference between the manager's assessment of the quality of performance and the individual's feelings about her own level of performance, it is critical that there be a common understanding.

Seek clarification for any assessments or examples that are unclear. Too often the individual feels as if she should simply be the silent recipient of the manager's discussion of her performance. That's a mistake. Although the manager will make the ultimate decision about the performance rating, it is very appropriate for the individual to expect that the manager will back up each of his assessments with examples and illustrations of the performance under discussion.

Consider how the appraiser's feedback will influence your performance plan for the upcoming appraisal period. Once the individual has a good understanding of the manager's assessment of her performance—and the thought processes the manager used to determine the rating level assigned—the individual needs to put that information to use. How will she approach new projects now that she understands how her boss looks at the way she goes about doing them? Which competencies are the most important? As far as the manager is concerned, is it better to miss a deadline to ensure the highest possible quality, or is it better to meet every deadline even if a little quality has to be sacrificed? The more the individual can learn about the way the manager goes about assessing performance, the more she can use that information to not only do a better job, but be seen by her boss as an outstanding performer.

Listen and respond appropriately to the appraiser's perceptions and feedback. The performance review is a discussion, not a lecture. Both parties must be active participants for them—and the organization—to get all of the potential benefit from the process.

5.4   What should I do before the meeting?

Here's a quick assessment tool to help you effectively prepare for the performance-review meeting:

Pre-Meeting Activities Checklist

- ☐ Gather information and materials.
- ☐ Choose a convenient time.
- ☐ Pick an appropriate place.
- ☐ Consider facilities and room arrangement.
- ☐ Determine the agenda.
- ☐ Give the individual a copy of the appraisal to read in advance of the meeting.
- ☐ Arrange for work coverage.
- ☐ Plan the way you want the meeting to go.

Tell Me More

Gather information and materials. The most important item you need to have is, of course, a copy of the individual's performance appraisal. But that's not all.

At the beginning of the year you and the individual had a performance-planning meeting. The individual should have taken notes on a blank copy of the appraisal form and made a copy for you. That document has all of the key items that you discussed during the meeting : Be sure you have a copy of that planning document in case a question about the original goals comes up.

You'll also need information about the individual's performance, particularly if there are some areas where the performance varied significantly from your expectations. Whether the variation was in a positive or negative direction, you'll need to be able to demonstrate why you assigned the rating that you did. If the assessment is that the individual's performance was less than you desired, it is then critically important that you have all of the evidence you used to come to that unacceptable or fair appraisal rating.

You may want to have a copy of the individual's development plan. You may want to have copies of weekly reports that the individual submitted that described progress against the goals that were set.

What are the key points that you want to cover during the discussion? In addition to having a copy of the appraisal, write down a list of the most important items you want to discuss. It's easy to refer to them during the meeting to make sure that everything that needs to be discussed gets covered.

You can't make a mistake by having too much support material. It will prevent the embarrassment of being unable to find anything of substance to justify the rating you gave.

Choose a convenient time. When is the best time to hold a performance appraisal discussion? There isn't any one particular time that is ideal—mornings or afternoons, early or late in the week, it doesn't matter. What does matter is having *enough* time. Wise managers set a specific time for a performance review—perhaps sixty minutes—and announce at the beginning of the meeting just how long they have budgeted for the discussion. They also make sure that the next activity scheduled for after the appraisal discussion is one that is either a low-priority (so that it can be rescheduled) or highly flexible (like working on a long-range plan). It may turn out that more time is needed to discuss some sensitive items that arise during the discussion. It may also be that the performance appraisal discussion turns into a highly creative brainstorming session that needs to continue beyond the one-hour schedule. Make sure there's enough time for unexpected events to play out.

Pick an appropriate place. Probably most performance appraisal discussions take place in the manager's office, with the manager behind the desk and the appraisee sitting directly in front of it.

Is that the best place to hold the discussion? It may well be, particularly if the appraisal is not very good and the manager wants to trot out all of the power and authority available to make the subordinate understand that immediate change is necessary. But too often the authoritarian, boss-behind-the-desk arrangement emphasizes the power relationship at a time when a more collegial approach might be more effective.

More important than the actual location where the discussion ends up is the decision-making process the manager engages in to determine that location. Too often, managers conduct the appraisal discussion behind their desks by default—they haven't given any thought to the matter and just let it happen in the place where they are most comfortable.

Consider facilities and room arrangement. There are several other alternatives possible. The manager's office might not offer complete privacy, particularly if walls are thin or it's a cubicle arrangement. In this case a conference room or the temporarily vacant office of an out-of town senior manager might be pressed into service. If the appraisal contains good news and the two participants in the appraisal drama are old colleagues, it might best be conducted over a cup of coffee in the cafeteria. And if it is conducted in the manager's office, just a little furniture rearrangement might reduce the hierarchical nature of the discussion.

If the performance appraisal does indeed contain bad news, and particularly if the manager believes that it will take a dramatic gesture to bring home the message of "change or else," the appraiser's boss's office might be a good location. Having your boss give you your performance appraisal in her boss's office—with her boss sitting in as an observer/reinforcer—certainly communicates the seriousness of the message being delivered.

But beware the unusual location. The district sales manager who gives one of her sales reps his annual performance appraisal while the two of them are in the car, driving down the highway en route to a new prospect's office, is exercising bad judgment. So, too, is any manager who selects a location significantly away from a business setting, unless the necessity for conducting the performance review at that time, in that location is obvious to both players.

Determine the agenda. How are you going to kick off the discussion? What are the first words you plan to say? Will you review the performance appraisal section by section, or do you want to start with the final rating and move backward from there? When are you going to review the employee's self-appraisal?

All of these questions will be answered by the time the performance review is completed. Too often, though, they are answered simply because "it just happened that way"—the manager gave no thought to the sequence of events that he wanted to follow.

A better approach is to have an agenda for the meeting. The agenda need not be written down (although that would be a good idea), but the manager needs to decide in advance how he wants to conduct the discussion.

Give the individual a copy of the appraisal to read in advance of the meeting. Before I became a consultant, I spent fifteen years working for three large corporations: General Electric, United Airlines, and PepsiCo. Each one of those companies had a rigorous performance appraisal system; each of my bosses took the process seriously.

But each one of my bosses followed the same clumsy procedure when the day came for my performance appraisal discussion. At the time we had set for the meeting, I would walk into his office and sit down. He would hand me the appraisal. I would crank up all of my speed-reading skills and whip through the multipage document just as fast as I could, eager to see all of the things my boss had said about me (probably missing a lot of the subtlety and nuance as I raced through it). My boss, meanwhile, sitting behind his desk, would make believe that he was involved in doing something important while I was reading, but it was obvious that his antennae were out, surreptitiously glancing at me, trying to gauge from my reactions how I was taking it.

What a bumbling way to start the meeting!

Here's a far better way to get the meeting off to an efficient, business-like start. An hour or two before the appraisal meeting is scheduled to start, get together with Sam. Hand him the performance appraisal. Say, "Sam, at 1:30 this afternoon we're going to get together for your performance review. Here it is. I'd like you to read this so that you're prepared for our meeting this afternoon. Feel free to write any questions directly on the form, or highlight anything that you want to be sure we talk about. See you then."

Sam now has an hour or two that he can use to read carefully what you have written, at his own pace. He can reflect on the things you've said without having to immediately defend or explain himself. He can jot down notes and think of questions he'd like to ask.

If you ask people to complete a self-appraisal, you can also ask for it at the same time that you give them a copy of your official appraisal. (That is, if you haven't asked them to send it to you earlier, so you can use it as an information source in completing the official appraisal.) You too will be more relaxed and better prepared by being able to read in an unpressured way what the individual has written about herself.

Red Flag

If the person you're appraising is a marginal performer with a bad rating, wait until the beginning of the meeting to hand over the appraisal. This increases your control of the situation.

Arrange for work coverage. If you don't have someone to answer your phone and you can't switch the phone to send all calls directly into voice mail, then make a firm decision to simply ignore any phone calls that come in during the meeting. Steal a "Do Not Disturb" sign from the next hotel room you stay in and put it on the door handle of the room where you're meeting. Tell your staff and colleagues to follow the "thousand-mile rule"—don't disturb you with anything unless it's of the same urgency that they would track you down and interrupt you if you were a thousand miles away.

Plan the way you want the meeting to go. There's a technique called creative visualization that professional athletes and motivational speakers claim to use. The night before a performance appraisal discussion, as you are drifting off to sleep, imagine yourself in the meeting with Sally. You see her walking into your office. You hear yourselves talking—not the actual words, but the tone of voice, the businesslike but friendly discussion.

You hear Sally ask you difficult questions; you hear your own voice responding confidently. You see yourself responding in a comfortable and untroubled way to the most sensitive issues that arise, as though you're watching yourself in a movie. As you finally drift off to sleep, you envision the meeting drawing to a close. Your confidence, poise, and self-possession are manifest as sleep finally overtakes you.

By visualizing success, so the theory goes, your unconscious mind will guide you toward its fulfillment.

5.5   Before I sit down to conduct an appraisal discussion with an individual, is it appropriate to talk with others to get some insights into what I might expect?

Yes. Once you have prepared the individual's performance appraisal and are getting ready for the discussion, there are several sources of information and assistance that can help you do a fully professional job:

- Your reviewer
- Previous supervisors
- Colleagues/customers/coworkers

Tell Me More

Your Reviewer. Your reviewer, usually your direct supervisor, is the individual who reads the performance appraisals you write before you present them to the individuals in your work group. In addition to reviewing what you have written, your reviewer can also be of help in preparing for the discussion. If there are areas where you anticipate disagreement, talk them over with your reviewer in advance and get suggestions on how to approach sensitive issues

A role-playing practice session just before you conduct a difficult review can be of great help in preparing you to do a challenging job. In conducting the practice session, make sure that you assume the role of the difficult employee and that the reviewer takes your role—the deliverer of the performance appraisal. In this way, you'll be able to see how someone else deals with the kinds of responses you may encounter in the actual appraisal discussion.

Previous Supervisors. Discussing your plans for a performance review with the individual's previous supervisor can be helpful, particularly if the individual worked for that person for a significant period of time. Discuss the key points you plan to make during the review and see if the previous supervisor encountered the same performance factors when the individual worked for her. Talk about the previous supervisor's experience in delivering performance reviews in case there are any insights or sensitivities you may not be aware of.

Colleagues/Customers/Coworkers. While it's not appropriate to review your plans for a performance appraisal with anyone other than the individual and your reviewer, be sensitive to the information you get from other people with whom the person you're reviewing regularly interacts.

5.6   How should I open the discussion?

The best way to put the individual at ease is to eliminate small talk and get right to the point. Here are some suggestions that will help you make the opening seconds of the meeting productive and comfortable:

- Welcome the individual.
- Describe the meeting's importance to you.
- Provide the overall time frame for the meeting.
- Tell the individual where you'd like to start.
- Describe how you'd like to proceed.
- Describe your plans for the planning meeting for the next appraisal period.
- Make your kickoff statement.

Tell Me More

The opening few seconds set the tone for the entire meeting. The following script incorporates all of the suggestions in the previously mentioned list:

> I've been looking forward to this chance to talk with you about your work last year, Mary. This discussion will be helpful to both of us.
>
> I'd like to go through the process slowly and carefully. This is one of the most important things you and I will do together all year. I have set aside an hour for our meeting, but we can spend more time if we feel it's useful.
>
> I want to start by having you tell me about the appraisal you wrote of your own performance—what you felt were the most important items and how you came up with the evaluation that you did. Then I'd like to talk about the appraisal that I wrote.
>
> The most important part of the appraisal form deals with your key job responsibilities and the goals that you set at the start of the year. I'd like to start there and spend most of our time together talking about the results you achieved. Then I'd like to look at the section that deals with competencies.
>
> I think the most effective way is to start by discussing those areas where you and I generally agree. Then we'll talk about those in which our views seem to differ. I'll give you my reasons, and I want to get your point of view.
>
> When we've completed that, I'd like to talk about my overall rating and how I arrived at it.
>
> When we're done, Mary, I'd like to wrap up by setting a date to get back together for our performance-planning meeting for next year. We'll update your key position responsibilities and goals, and also talk about your development plans for next year.
>
> Why don't you start by telling me how you feel this past year has gone . . . ?

In this sample script, the manager covered all of the key points. She came across as knowledgeable and well prepared.

There are certainly other items that could have been mentioned. For example, if changes in compensation are announced at the time of the performance appraisal, the manager might say something like this in his opening remarks: "As you know, the final performance appraisal rating affects the amount of merit increase employees get. I'm pleased to tell you that starting with your next paycheck you'll see a 4.8 percent increase. We can talk at the end of our discussion about exactly how that was calculated."

The better planned the opening few seconds are, the more successful the following hour will be.

Hot Tip

Note the manager's kickoff statement: "Why don't you start by telling me how you feel this past year has gone . . . ?" By saying that, the manager has put the conversational ball squarely (and appropriately) in the employee's court. The manager said earlier that she wanted to ". . . start by having you tell me about the appraisal you wrote of your own performance . . ." At the end of the introduction, she kicked off the actual performance appraisal discussion by asking the individual to begin by discussing her own views of her performance.

5.7 How do I start the appraisal discussion with an individual who has a great deal of experience and has worked for the company much longer than I have?

The process is essentially the same as it is with anyone else.

The fact that a subordinate is older—or younger, or a different religion, or a different shoe size—is irrelevant. Age, religion, and shoe sizes don't correlate with performance, and that's the only thing that the appraiser needs to be concerned with.

But appraisers sometimes inappropriately defer to the individual who has been around for many years—the old-timer who years ago bounced the CEO on his knee when the company's founder brought him to the office as a three-year-old child. True, longevity and organizational memory are virtues, but performance is what counts in performance appraisal.

The fact is that as the manager, you are the individual's boss. Even though Charlie may have been around since Noah and can tell you how things were run long before you were born, you have the responsibility of assessing and reviewing his performance.

Hot Tip

The best way to deal with the highly experienced individual is to get right to the point at the start of the appraisal discussion: "Frank, you've been through this drill many times before. Let's not waste any time on small talk. How do you think your department compares with where it was last year?" Then shut up and listen, and proceed as you would with anybody else.

5.8   It's easy to discuss the performance appraisal when the individual and I are in agreement. But what do I do when we disagree about something important?

Even when the manager and the individual agree about the quality of the individual's performance in one of the areas assessed in the appraisal, there are still some useful procedures to make sure that the agreement reinforces and encourages performance excellence. And when there's disagreement, several suggestions will make it easier to resolve differences and build a solid understanding:

For Areas of Agreement:

☐ Acknowledge the merits of the employee's reactions.
☐ Add additional information of your own.
☐ Point out where similar ratings are based on different facts or reasoning if this exists.

For Areas of Disagreement:

☐ Begin with your higher ratings.
☐ Proceed toward your lower ratings.
☐ Respond to employee's earlier appraisal.
☐ Give specific examples.
☐ State your reasons.
☐ Use active listening.
☐ Take extra time and care with sensitive issues.
☐ Remember John Dillinger's advice.

Tell Me More

Areas of Agreement. It's always easier to discuss a performance appraisal when you and the individual agree, particularly when the two
of you agree that the individual's work has been well done. But even
then it's important to continue the discussion further and not just let it
go at, "Well, we both agree that the Tompkins project was a major
success . . . let's move on to consider some other items."

Even when they agree with a subordinate's assessment that a particular project or goal was successfully achieved, wise managers probe
for the reasons the individual attributes to the cause of the success.
"What do you think caused that project to be such a success, Jim?" the
manager asks. Then she listens to see whether Jim's understanding of
the cause of the successes are the same as hers.

It may be that Jim's reasoning about the cause of his success is
different from that of the manager. Jim may say, "I think the primary
reason that things worked out so well is that I closely monitored each
of the decisions that the client made all the way through the project."
The manager, on the other hand, may acknowledge that close monitoring was a minor cause of project success but explain that, as she saw it,
a much more important reason was the recommendation that Jim made
early in the project that a cross-functional team be set up to make all of
the significant decisions during the course of the project. Explaining
her point of view to Jim will allow him to learn even more from the
success of the engagement, and—more important—will prevent him
from assuming that the cause of his success was a factor or condition
that the manager knows to be irrelevant.

Areas of Disagreement. In most performance appraisal discussions,
probably more time will be spent exploring areas of disagreement than
discussing those parts of the individual's performance where both parties agree that the job was well done.

Managers who are skilled at delivering performance appraisals
have learned to review the appraisal from the employee's point of view
before they sit down for the discussion. They ask themselves: Where is
the individual likely to agree with what I have written, whether the
assessment is positive or negative? Which parts are likely to provoke
disagreement? Which areas of disagreement will be resolved most
quickly; which will be likely to produce a significant amount of resistance?

In constructing the agenda for the appraisal discussion, don't start
the discussion with the item that is likely to produce the greatest

amount of disagreement. That's why, in the sample script of the opening for an effective performance review discussion, the manager said:

> I think the most effective way is to start by discussing those areas where you and I generally agree. Then we'll talk about those in which our views seem to differ. I'll give you my reasons, and I want to get your point of view.

That's a smart approach. As the manager, you're running the show. You have the right to decide what order you want to discuss items on the appraisal, as long as all of the items are fully considered.

Don't jump to the most contentious one first. Even in areas where you and the individual don't see exactly eye-to-eye, there will still be some areas where you are closer in your perceptions than in others. Begin with the easier items and move toward the more difficult.

Hot Tip

Another good reason for asking each of your subordinates to prepare an achievements list to begin the performance assessment process is that this list will alert you to areas where disagreement is likely to arise. If Harry writes down that his negotiation of the Smithfield contract was one of his greatest accomplishments for the year, and you know that the terms he negotiated were a disaster for the company, you are forewarned that this is an area where there is likely to be a significant amount of disagreement. Similarly, if Joanne's list of achievements is very short and contains items such as, "There were several weeks when I wasn't late to work once," you know that you'll be spending quite a bit of time during the appraisal discussion educating her on the performance standards the company has for its employees.

There is a magic phrase that leads to success in discussing performance, particularly in those cases where the individual's performance has failed to meet the manager's expectations. The magic phrase is: "For example . . ."

For each item where the individual is likely to disagree, make sure that you have some examples that support your less-than-ideal rating. The poorer the performance, the more examples you should have available.

The most convincing examples should be used in the written narrative itself. But be sure to have others available, so that during the discussion you're able to say, "In addition to what I wrote in your appraisal, Evelyn, I also saw some other areas where you didn't deliver the kind of customer service that we would like all of our product service managers to provide. First there was the incident . . ."

Active listening is critical in this phase of the performance appraisal discussion. The manager needs to state her rationale for the low rating, provide specific examples that support that decision, and then be quiet and listen to what the employee has to say. Frequently the employee's initial rejection of the manager's assessment may change once the person has had a chance to be fully heard and understood.

Restating the employee's position is a very effective technique. Responding to an employee's argument that a given appraisal rating is inappropriately low, the manager might say, "You feel that I gave excess weight to the poor result that we got on the client survey and not enough weight to the fact that you didn't have all of the resources that we might have allocated to the project?" Note that the manager is not agreeing with the employee that the weighting was inappropriate or that the rating was wrong. All the manager is trying to do is to gain a solid understanding of how the employee views the situation.

Restating the employee's viewpoint to ensure a common understanding will help prevent wasted time spent in arguing over a misunderstanding. Reflecting the individual's feelings can also help bring about resolution. "You feel slighted because you don't feel that I gave your projects as much attention as I did to those of other people in the department . . ." communicates that the manager has been listening closely to what the employee has to say and has the ability to understand and appreciate—not agree with—the employee's point of view.

Finally, remember John Dillinger's advice. Dillinger, the 1930s bank robber and most-wanted man, once advised, "Before you rob your first bank, knock off a couple of gas stations." His point applies to scheduling performance appraisal discussions: Before you hold the discussion with the individual whose appraisal review is going to be the most difficult, start off by conducting the reviews of those who have performed well and those where there will be little chance of challenge or argument. Build up your skills on the easy ones before proceeding to the most difficult.

5.9 How do I figure out what the employee is feeling?

Psychologists tell us that there are only four feelings: glad, sad, mad, and scared. All other feelings are variations on these four.

Glad is the feeling you're likely to encounter when you've given Tommy a great review. He did a great job; the performance appraisal reflects it. He's glad and it shows.

Sad is more common when the news is not good. The person is hurt and may react by becoming withdrawn. The voice level is lowered; the person is less animated and more constrained. Tears may flow.

Mad is the direct opposite of glad. The individual is angry, feels wronged. The voice level goes up, her face reddens. She seems ready for a fight. Interruptions are more likely.

Finally, some people react to a poor performance appraisal as scared. They are afraid of what will happen to them as a result of having done a poor job and having that poor performance become a matter of record. Their speech is hesitating; they ask worried questions about what will happen next.

Tell Me More

In each of these cases, reflecting feelings is a useful way to help the person deal with his or her emotional reaction to the performance appraisal and move on toward focusing on changes that need to be made to ensure future improvement. A statement like, "I get the impression that you're disappointed with the results of your performance appraisal, Charles," or, "You seem very worried about the assessment I have written, Paul," lets people know that you empathize with their feelings. It also lets them know that it's okay to permit emotional reactions in the discussion.

Red Flag

Don't ever use the phrase "I know how you feel . . ." in trying to reflect the individual's feelings. You actually don't know how the person feels. Rather, you are trying to understand. Saying "I know how you feel" is likely to provoke a spirited, "No, you don't!" Another phrase to avoid absolutely is, "You shouldn't feel that way." Although our own emotional reaction might differ from the one that the employee is experiencing, telling the person what his emotional reaction to a distressing event should be is inappropriate.

5.10   How can I get someone to agree with an honest and accurate performance appraisal rating?

You can't. Don't try.

Consider what the goal of a performance appraisal discussion is—and what it's not. The goal is not to gain agreement. If you gain agreement, that's fine, but it's unlikely if the appraiser has evaluated the individual's performance against tough-minded, demanding standards. In fact, the lower the appraisal rating, the less likely the individual is to agree with the assessment. That's okay.

The goal of the performance appraisal discussion is to gain understanding, not agreement. Whether or not the individual agrees with the assessment, or the factors that were used in making it, or the standards that the appraiser expects the individual to meet, the manager's job is to get the individual to understand the reason that his performance was rated the way it was.

Gaining agreement is nice; gaining understanding is mandatory.

5.11   The employee I'm about to review is an unsatisfactory performer and the appraisal tells it like it is. How should I start the meeting?

Get right to the point. As soon as the person arrives for the appraisal discussion, say, "Come in, George, sit down. I have some bad news for you. (Pause.) I have your performance appraisal here and quite frankly, George, it isn't very good." Then give the individual a copy of the appraisal to read. As soon as he has read it, begin the discussion.

Tell Me More

Communications gurus always advise managers to set the proper tone for the meeting. That's what you have just done in opening this meeting. You have advised the employee that the performance appraisal is not good and have prepared the individual for what he is about to read.

Being direct and candid right from the start is appropriate. There can't be any mistaking the seriousness of the discussion and there's little chance of misinterpretation.

Being blunt may seem cold-hearted or cruel. It's not. It's much crueler to allow a marginal performer to think that she's doing okay when in fact her performance leaves much to be desired. If the manager isn't blunt about her performance deficiencies, a host of problems may arise:

- The employee's marginal performance will drag down the overall contribution of her work group.
- The employee will be less likely to be promoted or to be assigned to interesting projects. If an honest manager pointed out her limitations to her, she has the option of correcting her performance or moving to another job that she can handle successfully.
- Others in the work group are likely to resent a laggard's being given a free ride. They may reduce their output and commitment, since the organization is sending a clear message that it tolerates mediocre performance.
- When the employee finally gets the ax, she's much more likely to cry "Discrimination!" since she's amassed a full drawer of satisfactory reviews.

5.12   What do I do when an employee disagrees with something I have written on the performance appraisal?

Listen to determine the source of the disagreement. Is it a matter of fact? (You wrote that the employee received a customer satisfaction score of seventy-nine, but the employee says that his score was eighty-three.) Or is it a matter of judgment? (You wrote that the employee's customer service skills were unsatisfactory, but she feels that her skills are terrific.) If it's an issue of fact, get the facts and make any corrections necessary. If it's a matter of judgment, ask the employee for additional evidence. Then determine whether that evidence is sufficient to cause you to revise your judgment. It rarely is.

Tell Me More

Most of the time, the appraiser has a reasonably good understanding of the areas where disagreements are likely to pop up in the course of the appraisal discussion. Before beginning the appraisal discussion, ask yourself, "What am I going to say when George disagrees that his performance on the Lumumba project just barely met expectations?"

Start with your higher ratings and move toward the lower ones.

Be prepared to give additional examples besides the ones you've included on the formal written appraisal. Refer back to the informal conversations you have had with the individual over the course of the year.

Use active listening as soon as a disagreement pops up. For example, phrases such as "Tell me more . . ." or "What else can you share with me about that?" or "Really?" can encourage people to talk more about their perceptions. Simply nodding without saying anything at all encourages people to expand on what they have said. It's not at all unlikely that the employee, allowed a sufficient chance to think aloud about what you have written, will end up saying, "Yeah, I guess I see what you mean."

Remember what your objective in the discussion is—and what it isn't. Your objective in a performance appraisal discussion is not to gain agreement. It is to gain understanding. If the employee agrees with you, that's great. But particularly if your appraisal is a tough-minded assessment of the fact the Charlie's contribution was only mediocre, it's unlikely that you'll ever get him to agree. What you want is for him to understand why you evaluated his performance the way you did, even if his personal opinion is different.

Red Flag

If you haven't had ongoing, informal performance discussions with the individual over the course of the appraisal period, then it's very likely that disagreements will surface during the review. That's another good reason for scheduling periodic, "how's it going?" discussions with each person on your team.

5.13   How do I handle those awkward moments that always seem to arise in performance appraisal discussions? For example, the employee who is silent, or makes excuses, or turns the conversation around so that we are caught up in irrelevancies?

Silences, excuses, and irrelevancies are the three most common discussion difficulties that arise in the course of discussing a performance evaluation. You can overcome each of these by keeping firmly in control with a few simple techniques.

Silences. Silences make us feel awkward. If the individual doesn't answer a question promptly, the reason may be that the person is uncomfortable or doesn't know what to say. It may also be a manipulative power play.

Silence can be used to intimidate. Make sure you're not the one who's being intimidated. Ask a question and wait. When your anxiety level rises to the point where you have to say something to break the silence, simply ask, "Do I need to repeat the question?" That will surely provoke a response. If it doesn't, call the performance appraisal meeting to a halt and explain what the word *insubordination* means.

Excuses. Excuses are the most common discussion difficulty. The reason we find them so difficult is that we typically deal with them so badly. We foolishly argue with the merits of the excuse, and by doing so legitimatize it.

While it may not be a conscious choice, any time a person offers an excuse for poor performance, the person proffering the excuse is trying to absolve himself of personal responsibility. Our response needs to focus not on the excuse but on the issue of personal responsibility.

Start by agreeing with the fact of the excuse: "I agree, Mark. Having deadlines that frequently change in the middle of a project does make your work difficult." Then put the responsibility back where it belongs: "And as we've discussed before, changing deadlines is a fact of life in our business. How are you planning to handle that challenge so that you can make sure that your projects are always ready when they're needed?"

The appraiser can increase the probability that the employee will change and resolve a problem if the manager discusses the need for change in terms of the choices the employee makes. We each have the capability for choice. An effective appraisal discussion makes that fact clear to the individual who might prefer to play the role of victim.

Hot Tip

It is always appropriate for the manager to consider in advance some possible approaches or solutions the employee might use to solve a problem. But the responsibility for finding a solution is the employee's; not the manager's. If the manager makes a suggestion that the employee accepts and it subsequently turns out that the suggestion was not effective in solving the problem, the employee can turn back to the manager and say, "See! I did what you told me and it didn't work!" So while the manager may assist the employee by making suggestions or offering guidance, the burden of actually solving the problem and improving performance is always borne by the individual.

Irrelevancies. A final discussion dilemma appraisers confront is the irrelevancy trap. All of a sudden, in the middle of a discussion, you realize that the subject you're talking about has nothing to do with the core issue of the appraisee's unacceptable performance.

Labeling an irrelevancy as such is unproductive. It only generates arguments. Don't waste your breath.

When you discover that you're in the middle of an active discussion of an irrelevant topic, the technique to use is "dismiss and redirect." Wait until your counterpart pauses for breath and then say, "As far as the way they used to handle this situation in your old company is concerned, I'd like to talk about that separately. First, I need for you to agree that you will let me know any time a project deadline is slipping."

The keywords are *separately* and *first*. The magic dismiss-and-redirect technique can be used anytime a conversational counterpart raises an issue that you want to make go away. You don't say that it's irrelevant, unimportant, or unconnected with the matter at hand. Instead, you graciously acknowledge its importance and then, with a sweep of misdirection, consign it to the nether world of irrelevancies and return to the primary issue on your agenda: "I appreciate your bringing to my attention the fact that the attendance record of other people in the department should be examined, Betty. I'd like to deal with that separately. First, I need your agreement that you will come to work every day on time." Or you may say: "I understand that many employees are looking for additional sources of income after the company announced the wage freeze last week, Carlos. But I'd like to talk about that issue separately. First, I need you to get your hand out of the cash register."

5.14 How do I handle defensive reactions?

Defensive reactions come in two forms: fight and flight.

Fight responses show up as angry rejections of what the appraiser has said or written. The individual may deny the accuracy of the appraiser's information or blame others for problems and shortcomings. Nonverbal indicators of fight reactions are usually clear: The person may pound the desk or point his finger. She may raise her voice or fold her arms defiantly across her chest. She may stare and refuse to engage in a normal businesslike conversation.

Flight reactions are entirely different. Here the individual's voice becomes quieter, not louder. She looks away, turns away. She speaks softly and agrees easily in order to change the subject. Where the individual displaying a fight reaction may discount any responsibility for the issue, the individual manifesting a flight reaction may take far more responsibility for a problem than the situation actually warrants.

Fight and flight reactions are hardwired, genetically based, normal human defense mechanisms for dealing with threatening situations. If your Stone Age ancestor stumbled upon a testy mastodon, his alternatives were flight, fight, or get trampled. Defensive reactions served a survival purpose. But they are out of place in the contemporary office.

Fight reactions are best handled by allowing the individual time to vent and encouraging the full expression of opinion. Most of these storms blow themselves out. Active listening is critical in dealing with fight reactions. Ask the individual for examples. Listen to what she has to say.

Hot Tip

In dealing with a fight reaction, your behavior should be the opposite of the individual's. As her emotional temperature gets hotter, yours should get cooler. As the employee starts to speak more rapidly, you should allow more pauses in what you say. If the individual's volume increases, you should lower your voice.

Flight reactions are subtler. The individual seeks metaphorically to flee the threatening situation. The easiest way is simply to agree with whatever is being said, change the subject, and move on.

The challenge to appraisers when flight reactions arise is to continue to focus on the performance deficiency until there is complete understanding. Too often, the appraiser is nervous about confronting Billie Jo with the fact that her performance was less than acceptable. But immediately upon being presented with the truth, Billie Jo says,

"Yes. You're right. I really did do a bad job this year. And I appreciate your bringing it to my attention. And you can count on me to do better in the future. I promise, I really will."

We tend to be so relieved about not having to go through an unpleasant confrontation that we accept Billie Jo's hastily offered, doubtfully sincere assurances and move on. But if we accept her statement at face value, it's unlikely that there will be a genuine commitment to change. That's why the effective manager says, "Thanks, Billie Jo. I'm glad we both look at it the same way. But let's actually go through analyzing what happened this year so that you can make some plans that will really make a difference in the upcoming twelve months."

5.15   How should I react when an employee starts crying during the appraisal discussion . . . or gets mad at me?

No manager should begin a performance appraisal discussion without a box of tissues handy. Crying is one of the most common ways in which a flight reaction displays itself. An employee's involuntary crying makes a difficult situation even more challenging. In this case, simply pull out the box of tissues, slide it over to the individual, give the person a few seconds to recompose himself, then carry on with the conversation.

Red Flag

Crying can also be a manipulative device, a way of extricating oneself from an unpleasant situation. If the crying continues beyond the point where it seems appropriate, or if the individual starts crying every time the manager presses forward to explore an aspect of unsatisfactory performance, you may be dealing with manipulative behavior instead of defensiveness. If this appears to be the case, say in a fairly stern manner, "Mary, we need to have a business discussion of your performance and the appraisal I have written about your performance. I understand that you may be uncomfortable discussing the fact that you are not performing at an acceptable level, but that is a requirement. I don't want to reschedule this meeting, but I will if you are unable to maintain appropriate business behavior. Are you ready to continue?" If the person continues to behave inappropriately, stop the meeting and discuss the events with your boss, human resources manager, or other senior individual. Then set up another meeting with a human re-sources representative or some other senior third party present. If the inappropriate behavior again is displayed, disciplinary action is appropriate.

If the employee becomes angry, tell the individual that you are aware of his reaction. Say, "John, you appear to be getting quite angry." Then wait for the response. In most cases, having someone else in a business setting point out that we are becoming angry is enough to cool things down. If this happens, as usually it will, continue with your discussion.

However, if the individual's response is to escalate the anger, or if he continues to justify his anger, explain that his behavior is inappropriate and that you will abort the meeting unless there is an immediate change. Let the individual know that there will be serious adverse consequences unless the inappropriate behavior ends instantly. Say, "John, your anger and shouting are not appropriate in a business setting. If you are unable to control yourself, I will end this meeting and call security. Are you able to continue?"

If the individual does not immediately change, walk out of the room and call security.

5.16   When should I talk about the pay increase?

Ideally, the discussion about compensation and the discussion about performance should be separate talks. If it's possible, the performance appraisal meeting should focus entirely on the individual's performance with discussion of compensation reserved until a later time. However, if performance and compensation must be discussed in the same meeting, begin with the compensation change. Then talk about the performance appraisal.

Tell Me More

In an effective performance management system, the individual's performance appraisal rating is only one of several determinants of the compensation change. Therefore it makes sense to concentrate entirely on performance during the performance appraisal discussion and wait until a later meeting to discuss Sam's pay increase. The way to handle this is to say, "Sam, as you know, the quality of a person's performance is one of the most important factors that the company takes into account in determining compensation. There are other factors, too. That's why I want to focus our discussion today entirely on your performance over the last twelve months and save our discussion about any pay increase until early next month."

In many organizations, however, it is customary to let the person know about a pay change in the same meeting that the appraisal is discussed. In this case, be sure to cover the pay change at the start of the meeting so you can get it out of the way. Say, "Sam, before we discuss your performance appraisal, I'm pleased to let you know that effective with your next paycheck you'll be receiving a 3.8 percent salary increase. Now let's discuss how you did over the past twelve months."

If you wait until the end of the performance appraisal discussion to reveal the amount of the increase, all of your words about the quality of Sam's performance will be drowned out by the little voice inside Sam's head that continually whispers, "How much . . . how much . . . how much?"

5.17   How do I bring the performance appraisal discussion to a successful close?

Here are the steps to wrap up a performance appraisal discussion effectively:

- Briefly summarize the entire conversation (review your core message).
- Discuss two or three areas of strength to be continued and enhanced.
- Review the most important area for immediate improvement.
- Explain the most important developmental need.
- Handle administrative mechanics.
- Schedule planning meeting.
- Congratulate (offer statement of hope) and close.

Tell Me More

After about forty-five minutes or so, both parties will start to realize that the major objectives of the performance appraisal discussion have been met and that it's time to start wrapping things up. Here's a script that will work in bringing the performance review meeting to a successful conclusion:

> Now that we've reviewed the complete appraisal, Mary, let's summarize the key points we've discussed. The most important thing I want you to remember about our discussion is . . . [Make a clear statement of the core message that you determined in preparing the individual's appraisal.]
>
> In reviewing the entire appraisal, there are two areas in which I think your performance has been outstanding. . . . [Describe two specific areas of strength that should be continued and enhanced in the upcoming year.]
>
> There is also one area in particular that you need to immediately work on improving. That area is . . . [Describe the single most important weakness or improvement need in the employee's performance and explain why improvement is necessary.]
>
> Finally, when you think about your development plans for next year, the one area I'd like you to give some serious thought to is . . . [Discuss most important developmental need for the next year.]
>
> That pretty well sums it up for me, Mary. Are there any other questions I can answer for you? [Answer any employee questions.]
>
> As a final matter, it's our policy to ask you to sign the performance appraisal to indicate that you've had a chance to read and understand it. If you'd like to add any comments, feel free to do so. [Give appraisal to employee to sign and cover any other administrative requirements.]
>
> This session has been extremely valuable to me, Mary, and I'm sure it has been for you, too. I'll look forward to discussing plans for next year on . . . [Set a date for a performance planning meeting to discuss next year's accountabilities and development plans.]

There's no formal requirement that you identify two strengths and one problem and one development need. It does make the job manageable, however, and it also gives the individual a reasonable number of things to remember from the conversation. If the employee can walk away having clearly heard the core message and remember just a few strengths and needs for change, you've done a fine job.

Hot Tip

It's appropriate to close the meeting on a positive note, even if the performance appraisal rating was unacceptable and the core message was that immediate improvement is required or termination will follow swiftly. Even in a case such as this, it's a good idea to end the meeting with a statement of hope that the problems will be corrected and the individual will return to the fold of good, solid performers.

Most companies' performance appraisal procedures ask for the employee to sign a copy of the form to acknowledge that the person being reviewed has had a chance to review the form and discuss it with the supervisor. Most also provide a section for the individual to add comments to the form. Both of these are good ideas.

Hot Tip

There is no reason that the employee should have to write her comments on the performance appraisal in the meeting with the manager sitting right there. Allow the individual some time—a couple of hours, a day or two—to think through her reactions and write the statement on the appraisal form.

5.18 What's the best way to deal with an employee who refuses to sign the performance appraisal document and refuses to provide his own comments?

It's unusual for someone to refuse to sign the form and refuse to put any comments in the section earmarked for them.

Start by asking why, and explain the purpose for the signature: "I'm surprised, George, that you are refusing to sign the form and also refusing to indicate any reason in the space set aside for your comments. As I explained, the purpose of asking for your signature is not to indicate that you agree with what I have written, but simply to show that you have seen this document and that you and I have talked about your performance. We have just done that, and I'd like you to acknowledge it. Can you tell me why you don't want to sign the form?"

If George offers no meaningful reason and continues to refuse, it's appropriate to remind him that the decision not to sign and not to put down any comments, like all of the other decisions one makes in life, will have consequences. "Frankly, George, I'm disappointed in your decision. You know that your performance is not acceptable and your refusal to follow a standard company policy only makes things worse. It's difficult for me to justify your being a member of our team if you refuse to follow reasonable company expectations."

Tell Me More

Dealing with employees like this one is frustrating. One manager wrote:

> Shouldn't every employer have as a policy that an employee's failure to sign and accept his/her review is unacceptable and can be grounds for termination? The employee can write his/her own comments on the form and express disagreement, but at the end of the day, it seems to me they need to accept the manager's assessment, move on, and work on the areas that need improvement. If there isn't a willingness to do that, isn't it just a waste of time to continue the employment relationship? One could probably go through the motions over the next six to twelve months and eventually fire the person for poor performance, but why drag it out that long when it's apparent the person just doesn't get it?

Red Flag

While it might be nice to consider George's refusal to sign the appraisal form as an act of insubordination and process the paperwork for his termination, it's not a wise move. Failing to sign an appraisal form is usually not considered a "culminating incident," and if George challenges his termination, he's likely to prevail. It's better to realize that you have a marginal and obstreperous employee on your hands and wait until the next incident of poor quality or quantity of work provides a genuine cause for termination.

Chapter 6

The Performance Appraisal Form

6.1   Is there an ideal performance appraisal form?

Yes. While the specific design and construction of the form varies from one organization to another, five elements should appear in every performance appraisal form:

1. Organizational core competencies
2. Job family competencies
3. Key job responsibilities
4. Projects and goals
5. Major achievements

Tell Me More

   1. *Organizational Core Competencies.* One of the hallmarks of an up-to-date, "best practice" performance management system is that it includes specific competencies that the organization expects all of its members to display. *Competencies* is the umbrella term that is used for all of the elements of performance that correlate with superior job execution and are predictive of success in organizational life. The term *competencies* includes behaviors, skills, traits, technical knowledge, proficiencies, attributes, and abilities. Organizational core competencies are the ones that the organization expects of everyone who picks up a paycheck, regardless of his job or her organizational level. Communication skills and results orientation might be core competencies that the organization has identified that it expects everyone in the company to demonstrate at a superior level.

   2. *Job Family Competencies.* Although there may be hundreds of different jobs within one company, there are only a small number of job families. For example, managerial/supervisory, sales, professional/technical, and operations all are job families. Financial analyst, lawyer,

computer programmer, and translator are very different jobs, but all of them are part of the professional/technical job family. Similarly, a second shift foreman and the senior vice president of marketing are both members of the managerial/supervisory job family.

Conceptual thinking and technical expertise might be competencies assessed of everyone in the professional/technical job family, while the competencies of people development and motivating subordinates might only show up on the form used for employees in the managerial/supervisory job family. Some competencies may be included as assessment items in several job families. For example, interpersonal skills might be a competency that is important for success in every job family.

3. *Key Job Responsibilities.* The competencies part of the appraisal form focuses on how the person goes about doing the job—the skills and proficiencies and attributes she demonstrates. The key job responsibilities section of the appraisal form focuses more specifically on what the individual is expected to do. If the organization has well-constructed job descriptions, these key responsibilities appear on each person's job description. More frequently, the language in the job description is less specific than is useful for performance appraisal purposes. In this case, the manager and the individual determine what the individual's key job responsibilities are during the performance-planning discussion.

4. *Goals and Projects.* These are the individual's activities that are beyond the specific tasks and duties outlined on a job description. For example, the key job responsibilities of a person holding the job of order-entry analyst will be the same no matter how many order-entry analysts there are, where they are located, or how long they have been in the position. But different order-entry analysts may have very different goals and may be assigned to work on significantly different projects.

5. *Major Achievements.* Every performance appraisal form should require the manager to identify the major accomplishments that the individual was responsible for over the course of the year. This section is frequently the place where the connection is made between the individual's performance and the organization's mission or vision and values.

Figure 6-1 illustrates the components of an ideal performance appraisal form.

Figure 6-1. An ideal performance appraisal form.

Focus

How (Behaviors)

Organizational Core/Cultural Competencies
❏ Limited in number
❏ Apply to all

Job Family Competencies
❏ Managerial/supervisory
❏ Professional/technical
❏ Sales
❏ Administrative, etc.

What (Results)

Key Job Responsibilities
❏ Source:
   Job description
   "Big Rocks" analysis
   Tasks & duties
❏ Focus–excellence in
   execution

Goals/ Major Projects
❏ Requires discretionary
   time
❏ Not appropriate for all
   jobs
❏ Focus–position
   transformation

Major Achievements

Source: Grote Consulting Corporation.

6.2 How does a company determine which competencies are truly core competencies?

Several studies have focused on identifying the various competencies that predict success, both in organizational life in general and in specific jobs or job families. My firm, Grote Consulting Corporation, has identified thirty specific competencies, based both on formal research (several of the research studies are described in my book, *The Complete Guide to Performance Appraisal*) and on thirty years of experience in helping organizations develop effective performance management systems.

There are many lists of competencies. Each list contains dozens of traits/skills/attributes—competencies—that can be picked over to identify the small number that are critically important. Whatever the source and number of competencies, the use of a competency process as part of an organization's performance appraisal process begins with the organization's choosing a small number of critical competencies out of dozens that are available. So the first step in the process is making up a big list of all of the potential competencies, then narrowing that big list down to the critical few.

Hot Tip

Who decides which competencies will be selected? The top brass does. Senior managers are charged with developing the organization's strategic plan and assuring its successful completion. Therefore, they're the ones who must make the decision about which competencies are the most important to achieve that strategy.

Tell Me More

Here's a step-by-step process for developing core competencies that will work in almost any organization:

1. *Get a list of competencies.* Make one up, buy a list, take one from various published competency lists. It doesn't matter. What does matter is that it be reasonably complete, containing all of the various traits, attributes, or skills that people in your organization might consider to be important.

2. *Make sure it's complete.* Show the initial list around. Ask people if there's anything obvious that's missing. Add everybody's ideas to the list regardless of quality. The weak sisters will be filtered out later.

3. *Write master-level descriptions.* For each competency you've identified, write a description of what a master performer would do in this area. Here's a key point: You are not writing competency definitions. You're not trying to define what the term means. Instead, what you are writing is a description of what somebody who's really terrific in this area is likely to do that ordinary folks don't do. Think about someone who genuinely is a model of interpersonal skills, or is the acknowledged expert on negotiations, or is terrific at customer service. What is it that she does that other people—ordinary mortals—don't do?

4. *Eliminate overlaps.* It's important to make sure that the statements used to describe the performance of a master apply only to one specific competency. For example, consider the phrase, "Easy to get along with." Does that describe the competency of interpersonal skills, or communication skills, or customer service, or people management ability? Take your choice, but choose only one. Never have the same description of master-level performance show up in two different competencies. It's important that the descriptions be sufficiently unique that no one can say, "Well, that's just the same thing in different words."

5. *Sort the list.* Once the complete list of competencies, along with the descriptions of master-level performance for each of them, has been created, it's time to assemble the top management group. Their task is to sort through the competencies and narrow the big list into the small number of competencies that are the most important. One fairly easy way to do this is to put all of the competency statements on index cards and give a set of cards to each person involved in deciding which ones are critical. The instructions are simple: Sort the deck of cards into three equal piles: must, should, and nice; or high, medium, and low.

Note that the instruction calls for three *equal* piles. That's important. It's also very difficult. If there are thirty different competency statements under consideration, the first time a manager sorts the list he's likely to end up with twenty in the must pile, eight in the should pile, and two in the nice, or low pile.

That won't work. The discipline involved in sorting the competencies into three equal piles is what makes the process work. If everything's a must, then nothing's a must.

Managers will wiggle and whine to avoid the hard job of saying that "developing talent," for example, is more important than "decision making," but less important than "planning and organizing." They'll point out that job requirements vary and that different people have various levels of skills. All of this is true, and all of it is irrelevant.

The objective is to identify the small number of genuinely important attributes, skills, traits, or proficiencies that give the organization a competitive advantage. Tough-minded decision making is required.

6. *Compare individual decisions.* Once each of the senior managers has sorted his or her own set of cards into equal piles of high, medium, and low, compare the decisions each participant made in order to come up with the final list. For example, it may be that of the seven managers participating in the card sorting activity, four of them put the "delega-

tion" card into the must pile, two put it in the should pile, and one assigned it to nice.

Mathematical analysis is not appropriate. Don't decide that the easiest way to sort things out is to assign three points to a must, two points to a should, one to a nice, and then let arithmetic prevail.

That's a mistake. You're not trying to solve an algebra problem. You're trying to illuminate the bone-deep convictions among the organization's senior leaders about what genuinely is important around here. What kinds of behaviors do they really want to see in the troops? Which important behaviors are they willing to sacrifice because others are even more imperative? Arithmetic alone can't give you the answer.

Instead, post the results where all can view them. Make up a flip chart with all of the competencies listed alphabetically and provide three columns labeled high, medium, and low. Then give each participant a marker and ask them—simultaneously—to put a check mark in the appropriate column on the chart to indicate their decision about each competency.

7. *Come to consensus.* Start by looking at the competencies that got the lowest number of votes, the ones that most people agreed belonged in the low pile. Pay attention to any fervent arguments from lone dissenters, but recognize that if most of the participants felt that "motivating subordinates" was a nice and not a must, that's probably the appropriate placement.

Once the easiest ones to eliminate have been discarded, look for ones where there is clear consensus that they are essential. If every participant put "visionary leadership" into the high pile, then there's not much argument about whether it should be included on the final list.

The difficult decision involves determining just how many competencies should be on the final list. This is a time when "the more the merrier" doesn't apply. Small is good. Fewer is better.

The objective of the competency development process is to focus the attention of every member of the organization on a small number of genuinely important attributes that top management expects of every organization member. The fewer the number, the greater attention that will be paid to each. Bill Clinton beat George Bush the elder by repeating, "It's the economy, stupid," not by saying, "It's the economy, and the Middle East, and school vouchers, and healthcare, and . . ." You get the point.

Exactly how many competencies should there be? Consider setting the maximum at seven. Most of us can remember a seven-digit phone number when it's told to us, but we often get befuddled if an area code is given, too. Actually, many of the competencies vying to make the final cut may actually be critically important in some jobs but not in others. Leave them off the list. For example, "visionary leadership" may be a critical requirement for success at the top of the organization, but not every pipe fitter or sales agent needs to display it.

8. *Publish and use the competency list.* Once the final list has been determined, make sure everyone in the organization is aware of it. Communicate widely. Describe the development process and why certain items made the cut while others didn't.

The most obvious and important place to use the organization's competency list is in performance appraisal. In many cases, the development of a competency list is initially undertaken as part of a bigger scheme to update the company's performance management system. If not, at least add the list of competencies to the existing performance appraisal form along with the descriptions of master-level performance. Then ask appraisers to evaluate how often the individual being reviewed performed as a true master in each area. Did the person display master-level performance sometimes, often, routinely, or invariably?

Hot Tip

Take advantage of any other opportunities for publicizing the competency list. Recruiting materials should tell potential job candidates that the organization knows exactly what it's looking for and what kinds of behaviors and talents are specifically sought. A copy of the list, along with the master-level descriptions, should be given to every new hire as part of initial orientation. The content of training programs should be reviewed to make sure that the critical competencies are reinforced in training.

6.3 Why is it better to write the narrative that explains what is meant by a competency as a description of master-level performance? Wouldn't a dictionary definition work just as well?

A definition provides a statement of the meaning of a word, phrase, or term, as in a dictionary entry. Although it may be useful to have a dictionary-like definition of a competency, what is really important is providing a description of what someone who is really good at performing this competency is likely to do.

Tell Me More

Let's take two examples of competencies that frequently appear in lists that predict success in an organization: accountability and teamwork. If you go to the dictionary, you'll learn that accountability means, "Liable to being called to account; answerable." You'll learn that teamwork means, "Cooperative effort by the members of a group or team to achieve a common goal." Both are accurate definitions; neither is helpful in guiding people on what they should do to excel in these two important areas.

Now consider a behaviorally based description of master-level examples of accountability and teamwork:

Accountability. Accepts personal responsibility for the quality and timeliness of his or her work. Believes that the results achieved directly result from his or her personal decisions and actions. Doesn't engage in behavior designed to justify and document decisions for self-protection purposes. Acknowledges and corrects mistakes. Doesn't make excuses for errors or problems.

Teamwork. Fulfills commitments to other team members. Promotes a friendly climate, good morale, and cooperation among team members. Puts team success ahead of individual success. Assures joint ownership of goal setting, group commitments, work activities, schedules, and group accomplishments. Lets other people finish and be responsible for their work. Doesn't hog the credit for others' work. Values all team members. Makes sure that the practical needs of the team are met. Protects and promotes the group's reputation with outsiders. Takes charge when it is necessary to facilitate an action or decision. Creates a feeling of belonging on the team.

There are four great advantages to writing competency statements as descriptions of master-level performance rather than simply providing dictionary-like definitions. First, descriptions guide performance by making it easier for the individual to understand exactly what is expected in each of these areas. All Harry needs to do is to read the description of accountability or teamwork and he will know what the organization expects in this area.

Second, it encourages development. By comparing one's current performance against the description of master-level performance, it allows individuals to see where they should be concentrating development efforts.

Third, it facilitates accurate appraisal. If the competency statements are written as descriptions of master-level performance, and the rating scale provided is one of behavioral frequency (e.g., regularly/frequently/sometimes/rarely), then it is easier for the appraiser to make an accurate assessment of the individual's performance in each competency area by describing how often the individual performed as a true master. The appraiser is not asked to make an absolute judgment about the goodness or badness of the employee's performance ("Let's see . . . was Fosdick fair, acceptable, or distinguished in his meeting of the accountability expectation?"). Instead, the appraiser is asked to describe how often Fosdick performed as a true master of accountability: Did he act this way regularly or just sometimes? That's an easier call for the appraiser to make.

Finally, it eases difficult discussions. It is easier for the manager to talk about the need for one of his employees to perform more often at a mastery level than it is to bluntly assess her performance as unacceptable. For example, let's say that Mary is not doing a very good job of assuring high quality in her work. Instead of having to say, "Mary, in the area of 'quality management' I rated you as unsatisfactory (the lowest rating on the appraisal form)," the manager can say, "Mary, in the area of 'quality management' I see you performing as a master occasionally (again, the lowest rating on the form). What do you need to do so that the next time we review your performance I'll be able to report that I see you performing as a master frequently or consistently?" Both statements about Mary's performance are accurate—she has been rated in the bottom category as far as her quality management is concerned. But it will be easier for the manager to encourage a thoughtful discussion about how she plans to develop her quality management skills by telling her that he sees her performing as a master only occasionally than it will be if the manager simply labels her performance as unacceptable.

6.4 What's the difference between organizational core competencies and job family competencies?

Organizational core competencies are those behaviors or attributes that the company expects to see demonstrated by everyone who is employed, regardless of that person's job or level. Sometimes called cultural competencies, these are the small number of skills, talents, and abilities that senior management has decided are truly core to the successful operation of the business.

Job family competencies are those that apply more specifically to some types of jobs but not necessarily to others. For example, "people management" is a competency that might be used to assess the performance of people whose job primarily involves supervising and directing the work of others. It's easy to see from the description that only people with supervisory responsibility can be held accountable for this area:

People Management. Regularly reviews performance and holds timely performance appraisal discussions. Hires the best people available. Doesn't hesitate to select strong subordinates. Has a nose for talent. Is watchful for subordinates and coworkers who appear to be having personal problems or concerns and encourages them to seek help. Knows people's career goals and helps them achieve them. Actively seeks development opportunities for employees. Holds people accountable and takes corrective action when necessary. Encourages and rewards effort, hard work, and results. Actively works to promote high performers and remove noncontributors.

Similarly, "safety" is a competency that will probably be included only in the performance appraisal of people in the operations job family:

Safety. Performs work in a safe manner at all times. Assesses the work site for hazards. Maintains an organized work area. Identifies and corrects unsafe situations. Plans a job with safety concerns in mind. Seeks guidance from supervisor and safety coordinator if needed. Attends and actively participates in safety training events. Considers the safety of other employees on the job site. Maintains personal protection equipment. Understands safety regulations and why they are important. Reports unsafe conditions. Communicates organization's safety policy to contractors and other nonemployees. Responds effectively to safety and health emergencies.

Does this mean that the organization is only concerned that operations people work safely and that everyone else can flaunt safety standards? Of course not. What it does mean is that safety is a core requirement in most operations jobs, while in other positions it is not an area of primary concern.

Tell Me More

There are some competencies that may appear in the performance appraisals of several job families. "Judgment and problem solving" is a good example:

Judgment and Problem Solving. Quickly grasps both the obvious and the underlying aspects of situations and problems. Looks beyond the obvious and doesn't stop at the first answer. Seeks advice from people who have successfully solved similar problems. Thinks through possible benefits, potential problems, and unintended consequences that might arise from variations from standard procedures. Helps others use reasoning and evidence rather than unsupported opinion. Others run their plans by him/her for reaction.

Obviously, the kinds of judgments that a systems analyst is required to make differ from those confronting a lathe operator. The decisions that the vice president of strategic planning has to make significantly differ from those her secretary has to make. But judgment is required in all of these jobs, and problem solving is a critical success factor in many job families.

6.5 How do I determine the key job responsibilities of a position?

Start with the job description. Most job descriptions include a summary of the most important duties and responsibilities of the position. If the job description isn't useful (or if there hasn't been a job description prepared for the position), then the manager and the individual need to discuss and identify the big rocks of the job—the half dozen or so most important tasks, duties, outcomes, or responsibilities of the position.

The easiest way to go about identifying the most important responsibilities of a position is to think about the big rocks of the job. Every person in an organization is involved in dozens of different activities over the course of a day. Whatever the job, it's the unusual one that only requires the repetitive performance of a limited number of tasks in an eight-hour period. But all of these tasks and activities are done in the service of a small number of key responsibilities—the big rocks of the job. Chapter 2 provides a detailed description of how to identify the key job responsibilities of a job using the "big rocks" approach.

Hot Tip

One great benefit of taking the big rocks approach to identifying key responsibilities is that during the year, if an employee becomes involved in activities that depart from the mainstream of the position, she can ask herself, "Which of my key job responsibilities does this activity support?" If the activity doesn't support any of the key responsibilities, then it's time for her either to eliminate that activity from her day-to-day endeavors, or talk to her boss about the fact that she has a new key responsibility that should be included with the rest when performance appraisal time rolls around.

6.6   Aren't goals and projects part of a person's job responsibilities? Why does an ideal appraisal form have a separate section for goals and projects?

A goal or special project is a part of the job that an individual does in addition to meeting the key job responsibilities of her position.

There are two elements that make goals different from key job responsibilities. The first is the time focus. Key job responsibilities focus on the job as it is right now; as it is captured in a job description. On the other hand, goals are major projects and activities that focus beyond the existing job responsibilities. They may transform the job from what it is today to something new.

The other element that distinguishes goals from key job responsibilities is the concept of "discretionary time." To work on a goal, or to be involved with a major project, the individual must have some free time. If the individual's time at work is expected to be devoted 100 percent to the items laid out in the job description, then the individual has no discretionary time to apply toward achieving a goal.

Tell Me More

Consider a person doing a telemarketing job. The person comes in to work and goes to his workstation. He puts on the headset, brings up the list of names to call on his computer screen, dials the first number, and as soon as the target has answered, goes into the pitch. Spends eight hours a day dialing for dollars; goes home. There is no discretionary time in that job and therefore little opportunity for meaningful goal setting. The entire focus of the telemarketer's job is to call and sell, call and sell.

6.7 The last part of the recommended performance appraisal form covers the individual's major accomplishments over the course of the appraisal period. Shouldn't the individual's achievements be described throughout the appraisal form?

Yes. For anyone other than a marginal performer, the appraisal should place the emphasis on identifying and reinforcing the strengths the person demonstrated over the course of the appraisal period.

Tell Me More

There are two reasons for having a separate section at the end in which the appraiser is asked to identify a specific and small number of critical achievements by the individual over the course of the year. First, it forces the manager to actually think about what the individual's most important achievements were. Most people in an organization do a good job. But what were the unique and particular contributions that Betty made over the course of the year that were head and shoulders above the rest of what she accomplished? It's appropriate for managers to have to think specifically about that question and develop a limited number of answers.

Second, a section like this at the end of the form is an ideal place for the company's mission statement, or its vision and values statement, and also for the most important contributions that the individual made to support that mission or demonstrate those values. For example, in the performance appraisal form of the Minnesota Department of Transportation, the last section instructs appraisers as follows: "In the following section list the individual's three to four most important achievements during the appraisal period. Consider what he or she did to help Mn/DOT develop a coordinated transportation network by safeguarding what exists, making the network operate better, and making Mn/DOT as a whole more effective/user-friendly/safe." These words are lifted directly from Mn/DOT's mission statement. Having them as the final appraisal element reinforces the importance of the agency's mission and makes a close connection between Mn/DOT's reason for existence and its performance expectations of all its employees.

6.8   Are there any other elements that could be included on a performance appraisal form?

Yes. There are several other elements or sections that might be included in the performance appraisal form:

- Demographic data
- Instructions for completion
- Attendance record
- Development plans and goals
- Approvals
- Appraiser summary
- Employee comments
- Promotability and potential analysis
- Signatures

Tell Me More

Demographic Data. Obviously the form must contain the name of the individual, the name of the appraiser, and the date of the appraisal. Besides these three components, there are several other pieces of demographic data that might appear on the front cover of the form, including:

- Job title
- Division/department/work unit identifier
- Social Security number
- Pay grade or salary classification
- Evaluation period
- Length of time the appraiser has supervised the individual
- The individual's start date with the organization
- Reason for appraisal (e.g., regular annual, employee request, voluntary transfer, involuntary transfer, probationary)

- Current salary and position in range
- Date of midcycle performance review
- Date of next scheduled appraisal

Instructions for Completion. Ideally, all appraisers would have the opportunity to attend a performance appraisal training program before using the system. Yet even if this is true, there is still a benefit to publishing a brief set of instructions as part of the form that guides the appraiser through the most important requirements of developing and delivering a performance appraisal.

Attendance Record. Attendance is primarily an issue with employees in the administrative, operations, and clinical job families. If attendance is a significant issue, the appraisal form might include a statement of the organization's attendance expectation. For example:

> Comes to work every day. Is fully prepared and ready to work at beginning of work schedule and continues until the work day is done. Makes appropriate arrangements when adverse weather or other problems might delay on-time arrival. Conforms to work hours and schedule. Notifies others immediately when unexpected problems cause absence, lateness, or the need to leave early.

If the expectation is clearly laid out in the performance appraisal, the supervisor may also be asked to indicate how frequently the employee demonstrates master-level performance: always/frequently/sometimes/occasionally.

More important than the supervisor's judgment about how good or bad the individual's attendance record is are the actual attendance data themselves. The section on attendance should include sections for the following information to be entered:

- Number of days absent in the past twelve months
- Number of incidents of absence in the past twelve months
- Number of days late in the past twelve months
- Personal attendance percentage
- Organizational (or departmental) attendance percentage

One of the great failings of most appraisal instruments is that they fail to ask for the exact data about the individual's attendance record and instead merely ask for the supervisor's judgment about the extent of the individual's dependability.

If encouraging regular attendance is a significant issue for the organization, the use of a section similar to the above on the performance appraisal can dramatically highlight the urgency of the issue.

Hot Tip

Far more important than the number of days absent or late is the employee's attendance percentage compared with the organizational (company or department or team) percentage. Assessing attendance in terms of the individual's average absence rate greatly eases the burden of improving performance through coaching. The supervisor does not have to be concerned with the causes of absence or whether or not they were "excused." He simply has to request that the individual so improve his or her record as to be just slightly above average—a most reasonable request.

Development Plans and Goals. Most forms have a section for recording the individual's development plans; few of these are ever used well. If employee development is a serious concern of the organization, it should be addressed through a separate process and not just as an add-on to an already overly burdened form. If it is not a serious concern, eliminate any reference to development on the performance appraisal form. Development isn't performance.

Approvals. Accepted best practice calls for the individual's immediate supervisor to complete the assessment form including the final performance appraisal rating, then have it approved by the supervisor's immediate superior. It may then be forwarded to human resources for review and approval, particularly if notice of compensation change accompanies the discussion of the appraisal and almost certainly if the raise requested is outside any guidelines that have been established. Once all approvals have been collected, the form is returned to the immediate supervisor, who then schedules the meeting with the individual to review the appraisal form itself.

By using this approach, upper managers are able to provide a check-and-balance function to make sure that their perceptions of the performance of individuals two or three levels down in the organization are shared by those who directly supervise those individuals. If there is a discrepancy, they can discuss and resolve it with the individual's supervisor before the appraisal is discussed with the individual himself.

Advance approvals also give upper managers an insight into how their juniors go about the appraisal process. They are able to see how seriously they take it, how skilled they are in observing and recording performance, and how defensible their judgments about subordinates are. Finally, for inexperienced or semiskilled supervisors, the upper manager can provide coaching and guidance on how to conduct the appraisal discussion.

Appraiser Summary. In addition to asking the appraiser to identify the individual's most important contributions at the end of the appraisal form, many organizations ask the supervisor to close the assessment by writing a narrative summary that distills all of the information into a pithy paragraph or two.

Employee Comments. A section for employee comments is an almost universal part of almost every performance appraisal form—and a very good idea. Whatever the person may write, from a legal defensibility standpoint the organization is better off since it demonstrates that the form was given to the employee and he or she was provided the opportunity to respond. Handwritten comments from a terminated appraisee preclude the individual from arguing that the form was placed in the file without the employee's having seen it.

Promotability and Potential Analysis. Few organizations include an assessment of an individual's potential or promotability on the form. Indicating promotability on the form is likely to create immediate expectations of advancement if the verdict is positive and discouragement if the employee discovers that the organization does not see him swiftly ascending the steps of the hierarchy. Indicating an assessment of an individual's promotability may also lessen defensibility if a highly promotable individual ever turns sour, is discharged, and then challenges the termination.

Signatures. Every person who was involved in the preparation, approval, or review of the form should sign it.

6.9   How many different forms should there be?

In most cases, there should be one form for each job family in the organization. The organizational core competencies will be the same on every form, since everyone in the company is held accountable for meeting them. The job family competencies will vary with each of the different job families: managerial/supervisory, clinical, operations, administrative, sales, etc. The sections on key job responsibilities and goals and projects will be the same on every form, since these are essentially blank where the actual information about the person's responsibilities and goals is written in.

Tell Me More

It may be necessary, in unusual cases, to develop a unique form for a specific job that is both critical to the organization's success and significantly different from all other jobs in the company. For example, a company whose business was developing and managing apartment complexes created a special performance appraisal form for its resident managers because resident managers were the single most important factor in tenant satisfaction. A national food processing company created two unique forms, one for route salespeople and one for district sales managers, the salesmen's bosses. A third form was used by everyone else in the company.

Here's the opposite situation: The implementation team at Harford Community College decided that they would have only one performance appraisal form that would be used to evaluate the performance of everyone in the college, from the president to the groundskeeper. Their rationale was that they wanted to reinforce the importance of developing a "we're all on the same team" mentality. Having one form for everyone supported that purpose.

Hot Tip

In general, less is more. The more forms there are, the more administrative headaches will grow. Each additional form will increase geometrically the amount of administrative burden in managing the system.

6.10 How many rating levels should there be on the form?

The overwhelming majority of performance appraisal forms provide for either three, four, or five levels of performance. It is rare for an appraisal system to operate on the basis of pass/fail with only two levels of ratings. And there are some appraisal procedures that focus entirely on employee feedback and development with no link to compensation that provide for no final evaluation of performance at all. These too are rare.

It's also extremely uncommon for an appraisal instrument to call for finer distinctions than five levels. In more than thirty years of consulting with organizations on performance appraisal, I have seen only one form with six performance levels, another with seven, and one with nine (not including categories devoted to such issues as "not applicable" or "too soon to judge").

For the most part, unless there is easily quantifiable and numerical information, together with a clear standard of performance—sales results or widgets per hour, for example—a scale of more than five points makes a claim to precision which may be difficult to justify.

Tell Me More

The usual levels of performance used in appraisals are illustrated in Figure 6-2. This figure provides the arguments for and against three, four, or five performance levels. As the chart indicates, however, no matter how many rating levels are provided, appraisers always tend to use fewer levels than they are offered.

In most cases a five-point rating scale provides for sufficient gradations in performance to be acceptable to most raters. Three-level scales regularly become five-point scales, since raters can't resist putting notches between the three points. They find that some employees are better than satisfactory but not quite outstanding, while others are a little less than satisfactory but not quite unacceptable, so they add pluses and minuses to the form. Because three-point scales usually become five-point scales anyway, why not simply start that way?

6.11   What should we call the different levels? Does it make any difference whether we use words or numbers?

No matter how many positions there may be on the rating scale, the positions have to be labeled. There are four alternatives: behavioral frequency, verbal descriptors, comparison-to-standard, and numerical.

Figure 6-3 provides examples of all four alternatives including the various choices available for a five-level rating scheme. The figure also suggests the best way to use each alternative in a performance appraisal form.

(text continues on page 160)

Figure 6-2. Levels of performance.

Advantages	Disadvantages
Five Levels	
Provides for finest distinctions in performance More consistent with bell curve distribution Most managers believe they can discriminate among five levels of performance Consistent with familiar "A-B-C-D-F" school grades model Most familiar rating scheme—less training required	May be harder for supervisors to communicate how to attain higher performance levels Typically only four levels are used Middle rating usually perceived negatively, as average, or mediocre, or a "C student" May encourage central tendency
Four Levels	
Does not include a middle rating, which may be perceived as "average" Eliminates "central tendency" rating error May skew raters in a positive or negative direction Provides for finer distinctions than a three-level scale	May not provide a way to distinguish between those who can improve and those who should be terminated May skew raters in a positive or negative direction Typically, only three levels are used
Three Levels	
Supervisors find it easy to categorize performance into three categories Supervisors tend to be more consistent if given fewer choices—higher reliability Some jobs may be better appraised on a "pass/fail" basis Only three levels of performance can be proved empirically Middle rating implies expected performance, not average performance More consistent with TQM principles	May not provide fine enough distinctions in performance Managers frequently alter system by adding pluses and minuses Does not distinguish between those who can improve and those who should be terminated Typically only two levels are used Does not allow for identifying the truly exceptional 2–5 percent

Source: Grote Consulting Corporation.

Figure 6-3. Descriptor alternatives.

Type of Descriptor	Examples				
Behavioral Frequency [Best used for assessing performance against competencies]	Always Invariably	Consistently Regularly	Often Usually	Sometimes Occasionally	Rarely Never
Verbal Descriptors [Best used for assessing performance against key job responsibilities]	Distinguished Extraordinary Exceptional Outstanding Role Model	Superior Commendable Above Average Very Good Excellent	Fully Successful OK Competent Good Solid Performer Proficient	Needs improvement Fair Substandard Poor Adequate	Unacceptable Marginal Unsatisfactory Ineffective Not Acceptable
Comparison to Standard [Best used for assessing performance against goals]	Well Above Standard Far exceeds expectations	Above Standard Exceeds expectations	Fully Meets Standard Achieves all expectations	Below Standard Meets most expectations	Far below standard Fails to meet expectations
Numerical Descriptors [Best not used]	5	4	3	2	1

Source: Grote Consulting Corporation.

Tell Me More

As Figure 6-3 indicates, the best choice for assessing an individual's performance against the competencies expected of people in the organization is a behavioral frequency scale (e.g., regularly/often/sometimes/occasionally). To assess each competency, the most effective technique is to provide a narrative description of master-level performance and then evaluate how often the individual performed as a master.

When the organization is assessing the individual's performance against her key job responsibilities, verbal descriptors are the best choice. For example, in meeting her responsibility of managing the mail, was the secretary's performance marginal, fair, competent, superior, or distinguished?

In the part of the appraisal that focuses on goals, use comparison-to-standard descriptors. At the beginning of the appraisal period during the planning meeting, the individual and the supervisor probably talked about their goals for and expectations of the results that would be achieved. Now it's time for assessment. Did the individual far exceed expectations, fully meet expectations, or fail to meet expectations?

The only one of the four alternatives to actively avoid on the appraisal form is a numerical scale. Even though it's common for an appraisal form to use numbers, it's a mistake. The obvious reason for avoiding numbers is that people resent being classified in those terms. More important, the use of numbers provides an illusion of precision that does not actually exist.

Ineffectual managers like being able to use numbers because it allows them to avoid making hard judgments and instead lets them treat performance appraisal like the solving of an arithmetic problem. If there are ratings for various sections within the form and then one final rating, weak appraisers will want to quantify everything and then come up with an arithmetic average for the final rating.

That's a mistake. Not every part of the form is equally important, and a rating of superior on one aspect of job performance may not be as significant to the organization's success as a superior rating in a more critical area. Simply assigning a number removes the requirement that managers apply critical, tough-minded judgment to the performance of the members of their team.

The best approach is to use different rating descriptors in different parts of the form and not use numbers anywhere, with the conscious awareness that this will make it more difficult for weak appraisers to average things out in coming up with a final rating.

6.12   Should we use different rating scales for assessing different areas within the form?

Yes. No matter how many levels there may be in the final overall rating, it's a good idea to vary the number of levels and the labels or descriptors used for the assessments of different elements within the body of the form. For example, the section of the form that assesses the individual's performance against competencies might have a four-level, behavioral frequency scale (always/regularly/sometimes/infrequently). Likewise, the part of the form that assesses performance against key job responsibilities might have a five-level, verbal-descriptor scale (distinguished/superior/fully successful/fair/unsatisfactory). And there's no reason in the same form that the assessment of the individual's performance in achieving the goals that were set shouldn't be a three-level scale: exceeded expectations/fully met expectations/failed to meet expectations.

Tell Me More

Constructing the form so that the number of rating levels and the type of scale change as the areas being assessed change forces raters to think specifically about the exact quality of the individual's performance. It also precludes raters from adding up individual ratings from different places on the form and using those interim ratings to calculate an average score as a final rating.

If you do vary the number of levels used in the form, weak managers will complain that using different scales within the same form makes it more difficult for them to average out the ratings on various parts of the form in order to generate a final rating. That's okay. They will just have to work a little harder. Determining a subordinate's final performance appraisal rating is one area where it's important for managers to work hard.

Hot Tip

Albert Einstein once said, "The solution to any problem should be as simple as possible, but no simpler." There is a risk in making it too easy for raters to come up with a final appraisal rating by just treating the process as a math problem where they calculate the average score of all the ratings in various parts of the form and accept that as the final rating.

6.13   Should the form provide for putting different weights on the various sections?

Some objectives are more important than others. And some sections of the form may be more important than others. For example, although most managers would feel that both competencies and objectives are important, it is more important to do a better job at producing results than it is to do a good job in demonstrating the competencies. Obviously, not all objectives are of equal importance to the organization. Should the form reflect the fact that some objectives are more critical than others?

Weighting is a matter best left up to the manager and the individual to discuss during the performance-planning discussion. Trying to provide for predetermined weights for various sections of the performance appraisal form that will apply to a broad range of jobs is probably not going to be useful.

Tell Me More

During the performance-planning discussion, the manager and subordinate should discuss the relative importance of the items to be accomplished in the upcoming year. Although developing a specific index of relative priority might help the worker make good decisions when faced with conflicting priorities, the ultimate accuracy of these weightings is questionable. Individual situations that require discretional judgment cannot be predicted in advance (and the likelihood of a change in priorities during the appraisal period is high).

The primary benefit to specifying the relative priority among different objectives may be in providing general guidance to the subordinate on where he should concentrate his efforts over the year, rather than providing a formal multiplier for use in assessing the overall performance rating and recommending the resultant salary change.

If an appraisal form is crammed with predetermined weights, managers will be reduced to making statements like "Let's see, Fosdick, on your first objective I rated you as superior but since that had only a relative weight of .3 it becomes ultimately less influential than the 'barely meets standard' I assigned you on the second objective with a priority value of. . . ." This is foolishness. No value is gained through this exercise in managerial numerology.

Hot Tip

It is best to keep the weighting process simple and, if possible, optional. Assigning different weights to different objectives can indicate clearly that some are more important than others. Providing predetermined weights can also perform the more important task of highlighting objectives whose importance changes during the course of an appraisal year, or indicating the relative importance of key job responsibilities versus competencies. The best approach is usually to encourage managers to discuss the relative importance of varying performance factors during the performance-planning meeting. Managers and subordinates, in the course of setting objectives and entering them on the form, might be asked to provide no more than A, B, C, or high, medium, low indications of relative priority.

6.14 Should the form provide a recommended distribution of performance appraisal ratings?

In most cases, it's a good idea.

One of the most common problems with performance appraisal is grade inflation, where performance appraisal ratings creep up until everyone is rated as exceeding expectations. One way to counteract this problem is by publishing a recommended distribution of appraisal ratings, or requiring managers to conform to a specific predetermined ratings allocation.

Tell Me More

To start, recognize that a standard bell-shaped curve distribution of performance appraisal ratings, with as many employees getting higher-than-middle ratings as lower-than-middle ratings, is probably not appropriate in most organizations. For a bell-shaped curve to be mathematically valid, there must be both a sufficiently large sample size and a random distribution of elements being distributed. Although there are enough people in most organizations for the sample size to be large enough, performance in organizations is far from randomly distributed. People are not hired at random—organizations hire the best available talent. People are not promoted at random—companies promote their top performers. Organizations send people to training programs and arrange development opportunities to improve their performance. Why, then, would you expect a random distribution of performance appraisal ratings?

At the same time, we know that in every organization, some people do perform better than others and that performance overall distributes itself in a way that reasonably resembles a strict bell-curve pattern. The difference between a purely random distribution and the distribution of performance appraisal ratings in a well-managed organization is that in the latter there is an appropriate shift in the distribution of ratings in a higher direction.

If managers are applying tough-minded and demanding performance expectations to a talented and motivated group of employees, if these managers consistently provide coaching to help people improve their performance, and if they confront performance problems when they arise and quickly terminate those who are not willing to meet the organization's expectations, then it is reasonable to assume that more people will get a higher-than-average performance appraisal rating than a lower-than-average one. In this case, using a five-level ratings distribution procedure, a reasonable distribution might look like this:

Performance Rating	Percentage of People Who Typically Receive This Rating
Distinguished performance	Less than 5 percent
Superior performance	About 30 percent
Fully successful	About 50 percent or more
Needs improvement	About 15 percent
Unsatisfactory	Less than 5 percent

In the distribution portrayed above, more than half of all employees are expected to get the middle performance appraisal rating.

In most organizations, this would be appropriate. But twice as many people are expected to be rated in the category directly above the middle as will be rated in the one directly below it. Finally, a very small number of individuals produce results over the course of the year that are so outstandingly good or bad that they receive the ratings at the extremes.

If this is the ratings distribution that the organization would like to see, why not publish it directly on the performance appraisal form? In this way, everyone knows the expectations. It's an even better idea to let people know what the actual ratings distribution for previous years has been, so that people can see the degree to which the actual distribution resembles the desired one.

But should the organization demand that every manager in every area of the company follow this scheme? In most cases, requiring that an exact percentage of performance appraisal ratings be distributed according to a predetermined scheme is not an effective approach. If the work unit is small, managers will be required to rate people higher or lower than their actual performance warrants in order to fit the demanded guideline, and managers who have assembled a particularly talented crew (or managers who have inherited a work group almost completely staffed by slackers) will be limited in their ability to use the performance appraisal process effectively.

6.15   Some computer-based performance appraisal systems offer an electronic form with different traits listed: quality of work, quantity of work, attitude, or dependability. The manager clicks on a one to five scale and then the machine generates the text for the appraisal. Are these programs a good idea?

No. These programs are a very bad idea.

Tell Me More

These computer-based appraisal products provide the manager with a predetermined set of performance factors. The manager evaluates the subordinate's performance level on each of the factors, typically using a one to five scale. The software product then spews forth text that purportedly duplicates what the manager himself would write to describe Sam's performance at a "three" level for the trait labeled "cooperation."

All of these programs slight the critically important key job responsibilities and goals element of the performance management process, simply because it is much harder to provide assistance for these elements than it is to merely cook up a bunch of sentences that reflect various levels of performance for various traits. Another problem is that the most important part of performance appraisal can't be assisted by computer software at all, no matter how sophisticated: the quality of the meeting between the individual and the appraiser.

None of the packages fit any particular organization's culture. Each was designed to appeal to the broadest possible audience. The stronger the corporate culture, the less appropriate any of these programs is likely to be.

The sterile, machine-generated prose put forth by these programs is often excessively simple, repetitive, and insipid. Although these programs encourage managers to edit the language, most will probably accept the bland words as written.

Any personnel decision made that is based on the data from one of these programs will be very difficult to defend. Avoid using this type of program. It is a lawsuit-in-a-box.

6.16 Most people do a good job—not outstanding, not unacceptable—and therefore get rated in the middle category. But they all hate getting rated there. They see it as being labeled as a "C" student. How do we explain that getting the middle rating is not a bad thing?

There are four reasons that people hate getting rated in the middle. Three of them are correctable; one is not.

The one that we can't do anything about is the universal human tendency to inflate our perceived talents and abilities. One survey revealed that over 80 percent of American men believe that they are above average in sports; Lake Wobegon has become famous as the mythical town where all the children are above average. In the absence of persuasive data to the contrary, people always believe that they are in the "exceeds expectations" category.

Another reason that people feel uncomfortable getting a middle rating is the appraiser's failure to communicate performance expectations at the beginning of the year and provide informal interim and ongoing assessments during the year. If my boss says nothing to me about my performance during the year, then he must be happy with it, the individual reasonably explains to himself. And if he's happy, then I must be doing better than just okay. And if I'm better than just okay, then I must therefore be superior. There's nothing wrong with the individual's logic—the fault lies in the manager's failure to set tough-minded performance expectations at the start of the year and to communicate all through the year that meeting those demanding standards is "fully meeting expectations."

The third reason people resist a middle rating is that they see it as equivalent to school grades: A, B, C, D, and F. To get a middle rating means that the individual is considered an organizational C student.

That's not true, and the school grades metaphor is inaccurate. If anything, the appropriate "grade" analogy is to the grading system in graduate schools: A, A-, B+, B, and C. But even this analogy is faulty, since there is not a close connection between the evaluation processes used in educational institutions and the process used for human performance in organizations.

A better metaphor for the middle rating is shooting par in golf. Par doesn't mean perfect. Par also doesn't mean average or mediocre or middle-of-the-road, run-of-the-mill. What par represents is the number of golf strokes considered necessary to complete a hole or course in expert play. A pro golfer can often do better, but par is what is expected of an expert. The middle rating on a performance appraisal also represents the performance and behavior that an expert is expected to produce.

The most important reason that people resist the middle rating is that the terminology for the middle of the scale too often connotes mediocrity. If the middle rating is merely "competent," you can expect resistance. If the middle rating is only "meets expectations," you'll have a lot of disappointed performers. And if the middle rating is the worst possible choice—a numerical "three"—you'll get massive resentment and discontent. But if the middle rating connotes success, then it will be much easier to explain that being rated in the middle category is not the bad deal that it is often considered. For example, if the label for the middle performance category is "Good Solid Performer," who could object? If the middle rating is "Fully Successful," people can take pride in that designation.

Red Flag

The only organizations where the great majority of people are rated above the middle category are those where managers' performance expectations are set so low that even the village idiot can exceed them.

Chapter 7

The Performance Appraisal Process

7.1 What does an effective performance appraisal process look like?

As I described in Chapter 1, an effective appraisal process begins with a performance-planning meeting where the manager and the individual discuss the upcoming year, set goals, review the competencies that the organization expects people to demonstrate, and identify the key job elements. They may also discuss the subordinate's development needs and goals in this hour-long meeting.

Over the course of the year the manager and the individual regularly talk about performance. They adjust objectives as priorities change and as goals are met. The manager solves performance problems if any arise and creates the conditions that motivate. She also conducts a midyear review to more formally discuss the individual's performance halfway through the annual cycle.

Performance assessment is the third phase of an effective performance appraisal process. The manager evaluates exactly how well the individual has performed in each area covered in the appraisal instrument, writes narrative descriptions of the performance, and assigns the appropriate ratings.

Once the performance appraisal form has been written, reviewed, and approved, the employee and the manager get together for the final phase of the process: performance review. They discuss the manager's evaluation of the individual's performance and come to an understanding of what was accomplished over the course of the year and how those accomplishments were evaluated. At the end of this meeting, they set a time to get together again to plan for the upcoming year, and the process begins anew.

7.2   We're getting ready to design a completely new performance appraisal system from scratch. Where should we start?

Here is a ten-step process that works well in developing a new performance appraisal system:

1. Get top management actively involved.
2. Establish the criteria for an ideal system.
3. Appoint an implementation team.
4. Design the form first.
5. Build your mission, vision, values, and core competencies into the form.
6. Ensure ongoing communication.
7. Train all appraisers.
8. Orient all appraisees.
9. Use the results.
10. Monitor and revise the program.

Tell Me More

Get top management actively involved. Without top management's commitment and visible support, no program can succeed. Top management must establish strategic plans, identify values and core competencies, appoint an appropriate implementation team, demonstrate the importance of performance management by being active participants in the process, and use appraisal results in management decisions.

Establish the criteria for an ideal system. Consider the needs of the four stakeholder groups of any appraisal system: Appraisers who must evaluate performance; appraisees whose performance is being assessed; human resources professionals who must administer the system; and the senior management group that must lead the organization into the future. Identifying their expectations at the start helps ensure their support once the system is finally designed. Ask each group: "What will it take for you to consider this system a smashing success?" Don't settle for less.

Appoint an implementation team. This task force—a diagonal slice of appraisers and appraisees from different levels and functions in the organization—is responsible for developing appraisal forms, policies, and procedures and assuring successful deployment. Effective implementation teams usually divide themselves into two working task forces:

1. *Policies, Practices, Procedures (3P).* This task force is responsible for designing the appraisal forms and recommending policies and procedures. They also develop measurement systems to make sure the system is operating properly once it has been installed.
2. *Understanding, Support, Acceptance (USA).* This team works as a mini-advertising agency, arranging communication plans and programs to ensure understanding and support by everyone who will be affected by the system.

Design the form first. The appraisal form is a lightning rod that will attract everyone's attention. Design the form early and get lots of feedback on it. Don't believe people who tell you that the form isn't important. They're wrong.

Build your mission, vision, values, and core competencies into the form. Performance appraisal is a means, not an end. The real objective of any performance management system is to make sure that the company's strategic plan and vision and values are communicated and achieved. Core competencies expected of all organization members should be included, described, and assessed. If your mission statement isn't clearly visible in the performance appraisal system, cynicism will likely result. Values become real only when people are held accountable for living up to them.

Ensure ongoing communication. Circulate drafts of the form and invite users to make recommendations. Consider using focus groups to review ongoing efforts. Keep the development process visible through announcements and house organ bulletins. Use surveys, float trial balloons, request suggestions. Remember the cardinal principle: People support what they help create.

Train all appraisers. Performance appraisal requires a multitude of skills—behavioral observation and discrimination, goal setting, developing people, confronting unacceptable performance, persuading, problem solving, and planning. Unless appraiser training is universal and comprehensive, the program won't produce much. And don't ignore the most important requirement of all: the need for courage.

Orient all appraisees. The program's purposes and procedures must be explained in advance—enthusiastically—to everyone who will be affected by it. Specific training should be provided if the performance management procedure requires self-appraisal, multirater feedback, upward appraisal, or individual development planning.

Use the results. If the results of the performance appraisal are not visibly used in making promotion, salary, development, transfer, training, and termination decisions, people will realize that it's merely an exercise.

Monitor and revise the program. Audit the quality of appraisals, the extent to which the system is being used, and the extent to which the original objectives have been met. Provide feedback to management, appraisers, and appraisees. Train new appraisers as they are appointed to supervisory positions. Actively seek and incorporate suggestions for improvement.

7.3   What should top management, appraisers, employees, and human resources professionals expect from a performance appraisal system?

Each of these groups is a stakeholder in the development of an effective performance appraisal system. If their needs are met, they will be more likely to be active supporters of the system.

Not all of their needs and expectations will be satisfied simply by designing attractive and effective appraisal forms. Other needs will be met through the procedures that are adopted and the training that is provided as part of the implementation of the system. Finally, some of the demands that people have of a performance management system can only be satisfied through the actions of top management, individual managers, and human resources.

Tell Me More

Here is what each of the four groups of stakeholders is looking for in an effective performance appraisal system:

Top Management
- The development of a shared sense of mission by all members of the organization
- The ability to identify accurately the small number of outstanding contributors whose development and retention is critical to the organization's future success

- The assurance that lower levels of management reflect senior management's expectations of tough-minded and demanding performance standards for all organization members
- Accurate information on where the company is experiencing performance deficiencies and reliable recommendations on appropriate measures to correct those deficiencies
- The assurance that lower levels of management are accurately assessing the quality of performance of associates whose work they are responsible for, appropriately reinforcing those whose work is outstanding, and eliminating those who are noncontributors
- The assurance that the performance management process the organization is using reflects accepted best practices among America's most successful and sophisticated organizations

Appraisers/Managers

- Forms that are clear and easy to use
- Procedures that are sensible and easy to follow
- The ability to create and gain agreement on specific, challenging, and measurable goals
- The encouragement from top management and human resources to set demanding standards of performance and muscle-build the organization to achieve excellent results
- The skills to accurately evaluate—precisely and unarguably—an individual's strengths and weaknesses, particularly in hard-to-measure professional and knowledge-worker jobs
- The ability to discuss a performance evaluation in a way that removes defensiveness and leads to genuine change
- The ability to identify an individual's development needs and help that person come up with a workable plan that will increase capability
- The encouragement to confront noncontributors with the need for change and to terminate their employment if that change is not immediate
- The assurance that if an employee ever challenges the accuracy of a performance evaluation, the initial assumption of senior management and the human resources function will be that:
  —The manager acted correctly.
  —The burden of proof rests with the employee.

Appraisees/Employees

- Forms that are clear and easy to use; procedures that are sensible and easy to follow

- Clear communication of both the organization's and the immediate supervisor's expectations about performance so that they can make intelligent decisions about where to concentrate efforts and resources
- Ongoing feedback that reinforces appropriate actions and behaviors and redirects misguided efforts
- An emphasis on growth and development
- Factual and accurate performance assessments that allow the individual to make wise decisions about career direction
- The ability to influence the performance expectations and the measures for those expectations set by the manager
- Prompt communication when business decisions affect the priority of preestablished objectives
- Timely information about performance deficiencies and the opportunity to correct those deficiencies before they become a permanent mark on the record
- The assurance that the delivery of a high level of performance will be recognized in both formal and informal ways
- The assurance that marginal performance on the part of colleagues will not be tolerated by senior managers

Human Resources

- The ability to respond quickly and accurately to senior management's demands for information about the quality of performance in any organization unit
- The ability to monitor whether the organization's policies and procedures regarding the performance management process are being followed
- The assurance that performance management forms, procedures, and practices used by the company incorporate accepted best practices
- The assurance that all performance management practices fall squarely within legal guidelines and that exposure to legal challenge is minimized

7.4   What kind of training do managers need to do a good performance appraisal?

Depending on the complexity of the system, the sophistication of the managers attending training, and their previous management development experiences, conventional classroom-based appraiser training for managers requires between one-half day and two full days.

Tell Me More

Although the objectives and content of the training vary depending on the organization and the structure of its performance appraisal system, these are the knowledge and skills that any effective performance appraisal training program should provide managers:

- A complete understanding of the forms and administrative procedures, including the reasons for developing the new system and the specific design of the forms
- The ability to determine the key responsibilities of all subordinates' jobs and the appraiser's own job
- The ability to create and gain agreement on specific, challenging, and measurable goals
- The ability to create an infectious sense of enthusiasm and commitment to the organization's overall mission and the specific goals of their department
- Knowledge of the factors that actually generate motivation and the ability to use those factors to increase both job performance and satisfaction
- The willingness to set demanding standards of performance and to muscle-build the organization to achieve excellent results
- The ability to accurately evaluate an individual's strengths and weaknesses, particularly in hard-to-measure professional and knowledge-worker jobs
- The ability to complete the forms easily and accurately
- The ability to discuss a performance evaluation in a way that removes defensiveness, builds good working relationships, and leads to genuine change
- The ability to identify an individual's development needs and the skills needed to help that person come up with a workable plan that will improve performance
- The ability to identify that small minority of employees whose retention is critical to ongoing organization success and to apply appropriate retention tactics
- The ability and encouragement to identify that small minority of noncontributors and confront them with the requirement that they either change or leave

7.5   Do we need to provide training to employees about our performance appraisal process?

Yes. Although the training for employees does not have to be nearly as long or as detailed as the training provided managers (mainly because the skills required by the recipient of a performance appraisal are quite different from the skills required by an appraiser), it's a good idea to hold a training or orientation program for all employees to introduce the new system.

Tell Me More

Sixty to ninety minutes is an appropriate amount of time to set for an employee overview of a new performance appraisal program. In addition to the orientation presentation, however, it's a good idea to give everyone copies of the new forms, copies of the administrative guidelines and procedures, and perhaps a set of frequently asked questions about the new system and its design.

At the end of an effective employee orientation program, each non-supervisory employee of the organization should:

- Understand the reasons why the organization decided to develop a new performance management system
- Understand all of the elements of the form (e.g., organizational core competencies, job family competencies, key job responsibilities, goals, rating scales)
- Understand the specific benefits that a new performance management system will provide to him or her personally
- Understand how this program operationalizes the organization's mission statement and/or vision and values
- Understand his or her individual responsibilities in each phase of the performance management system
- Understand, accept, and enthusiastically support the focus on performance excellence encouraged by the program

7.6   Should we provide managers with samples of completed appraisal forms that they can use as models when they have to prepare performance appraisals?

Yes. This is one of the most effective ways to help managers do a good job. Surprisingly, only a small number of companies provide their managers with this high-payoff, easy-to-prepare aid.

Tell Me More

The best way to create sample performance appraisal forms is for a human resources specialist who is an expert in performance management to work together with an operating manager who is an expert on the job for which the sample appraisal form is being created.

Working together, the two of them should create a complete performance appraisal form for an imaginary employee at different levels of performance. In choosing the job for which the sample form will be constructed, be careful to choose one that provides a reasonable degree of challenge. Too often, when companies do prepare sample appraisal forms for managers to review, they pick jobs like secretary or human resources representative that are easy to describe and easy to explain. It's more helpful to managers to choose jobs that are more complex and sophisticated as examples, even though this will make the task of constructing the sample performance appraisal more difficult.

After the performance management expert and the subject matter expert have drafted a sample performance appraisal form, circulate it to managers and to people who actually hold the job that is being used as the example. Ask them whether they would come to the same conclusions about the performance ratings based on the data and examples in the completed example.

Red Flag

If the example constructed by the performance management expert and the subject matter expert is one of an excellent performer who does a fine job but gets the organization's middle rating, it's likely that reviewers will object, saying that they would have rated the performance higher. That's a good sign that ratings inflation is a problem in the organization. One of the more subtle but effective ways of toughening up raters' standards is to publish examples of excellent performers who receive appropriate fully successful ratings.

Hot Tip

In addition to producing samples of performance appraisals at the fully successful level, it's a great benefit to managers to be able to see appraisal forms that have been written to describe marginal or unsatisfactory performance. Too often, performance appraisal examples focus on people who do an excellent job. Although the majority of people in an organization may do an excellent job, that is not the group that managers need help with in sharpening their appraisal skills. Giving them examples of the written assessments of poor performers not only increases their ability to write similar appraisals, but also sends a message that this is what the organization expects them to do.

7.7   How can an organization determine whether its managers are doing a good job in performance appraisal and that the system is working well?

The single best test is that the organization gets 100 percent uncomplaining compliance with every procedural requirement of its performance appraisal system.

Tell Me More

There are many other checks the organization can make to be sure that the system is operating right. Here are some questions and issues to think about in evaluating the effectiveness of your performance management process:

- *Is there a significant difference between the ratings received by employees their first year on the job compared with the ratings that they receive in following years?* It is logical to assume that performance appraisal ratings will go up in a person's second and third year on the job as she gains more skill and increases in experience.
- *Is there a consistent distribution of performance appraisal ratings at various job or salary levels?* In other words, for all people at one level, what percent are rated in the middle category, what percent are rated superior, what percent are rated needs improvement? Is the percentage the same for higher and lower levels? In analyzing this, a reasonable assumption might be that as job level goes up (and therefore, we assume, training, skill, talent, etc.) we would expect to see a positive correlation between the percentage of individuals receiving a superior rating and the level of the job. If the reverse is true (i.e., lower level people are getting a higher percentage of superior ratings), it may indicate that senior managers have higher performance expectations of

more highly paid personnel than they do of lower level employees. Whatever the explanation, it would be good to determine the cause.

■ *What percentage of people received the same rating in year two of employment as they did in year one?* What percent got a higher rating (moved from the middle rating to superior)? What percent got a lower rating (moved from superior to the middle rating, or from the middle rating down to fair)?

■ *Is the distribution of ratings for employees at various levels reasonably consistent with ratings for employees in other divisions of the company at the same levels?* If there is a difference, are there data available to explain the cause?

■ *Are the overall performance appraisal ratings of employees who work in departments that are generally considered to be talent-rich, high-performing operations different from the average ratings of employees in departments that are reputed to harbor large numbers of has-beens and also-rans?* One might expect the average performance appraisal rating to be higher in a talent-rich department than in one that is filled with duds. Frequently, however, the reason high-performing departments and work units are that way is that the manager has high performance expectations and awards stellar ratings only when stellar performance is delivered. Too often, the higher the average performance appraisal rating, the poorer the overall performance of that unit.

■ *Is the face validity of the performance appraisal ratings distribution acceptable to top management?* For example, if 60 percent of all exempts are rated in the middle category, 30 percent as superior, and 10 percent spread among the other three categories, does that seem appropriate? Is the organization overall being too tough, too lenient, or about right?

■ *If one-fifth of all employees were to be immediately dismissed because of a corporate mandate to reduce headcount by 20 percent, is senior management willing to rely exclusively on last year's performance appraisal ratings in making the who goes/who stays decision?* If not, why not?

■ *Are there pockets of performance rating skew (positive or negative) within different departments or divisions?* Are some managers particularly tough or lenient evaluators?

Hot Tip

In addition to getting the answers to these questions, it is a worthwhile exercise to enter all of the data available into an electronic spreadsheet and play with the graphing function. A lot of times displaying data in a graphical format can help you see issues that raw numbers themselves don't make clear.

7.8 Both appraisers and employees are confused about what the different rating labels actually mean. How do we solve this communication problem?

Companies often think that just by providing a brief definition of each of the levels on their rating scale, people will thereby understand exactly what is meant by the term. That is not true. A great deal of confusion will result because people will apply different labels to indicate the same quality of performance.

The most effective way to communicate the exact meaning of each of the rating levels on a performance appraisal form is not to offer a definition. Instead, provide a narrative description about the message that each rating label is intended to communicate about the quality of the individual's performance.

Tell Me More

In Chapter 4, I provided an example of the messages sent by different performance appraisal ratings using a five-level comparison-to-standard scale. Here is an example of the message that is intended to be sent by each of the various rating labels that might be used in a five-level, behavioral-frequency rating scale:

Always/Invariably. The individual habitually acts as described in every area. Behaving in the manner described is ingrained in the individual's personal style and it would be almost impossible for him or her not to perform every one of the actions exactly as described. People would notice and remark if the individual ever acted in any way other than the way described.

Regularly/Consistently. This is the individual's normal and preferred method of operation, although at unusual times, variations may occur. Acting as a master performer as described in the narrative is a recurrent and normal pattern in the individual's choice of behavior.

Often/Usually. The individual mostly acts in the way of a master performer in the area, but variations arise in times of stress or pressure. While many—or most—of the descriptions of mastery performance are common in the individual's performance, there are some areas where the person acts in ways that need development.

Occasionally/Sometimes. From time to time the individual acts as a master would in this area, but a common pattern has not been established. It is difficult to predict in any given situation whether the person will act as described in the narrative. The behaviors described in the narrative are a now-and-then, once-in-a-while, periodic pattern.

Rarely/Never. Master-level performance in this area is occasionally seen, but it is seldom and not habitual. The individual may from time to time act as a master performer, but it is not the individual's usual style and would be seen by others as the exception rather than the rule. While the person may have the capability to perform at a master-level with regard to many of the indicators, actually doing so is an occasional and infrequent occurrence.

Hot Tip

Publishing these descriptions of the message that is inherent in each of the performance ratings is also a very effective way to let people know that the middle rating is not average or mediocre and that the higher ratings genuinely involve remarkable levels of performance.

7.9 Managers don't seem to understand all the things that they need to do and end up waiting until the last minute to meet their performance appraisal activities. Human resources then ends up playing policeman. What can HR do to help them do a better job?

The easiest way to avoid being tagged with the "policy cop" role (although it is an important and appropriate one) is to provide managers with workable tools that will help them understand the whole process and what their responsibilities are. One way to do this is by providing them with a checklist that indicates all of the system requirements and allows them to track their progress in meeting the requirements. Here is a sample:

Date	Activity	Completed?
March 1	Identify the number of people for whom you will have to complete annual performance appraisals for this year. Consider: ☐ Current direct reports ☐ Transferred or promoted individuals who worked for you for more than three months ☐ Individuals who directly report to another manager but for whom you are a primary source of performance information	☐
March 8	Determine the date on which you will attend the performance appraisal training program in Atlanta. (Training programs will be conducted on May 1, 4, and 9.)	☐
March 9	E-mail your training program reservation request to Joe Smith at headquarters. Send to: *smith@headquarters.com*	☐
March 14	Review your performance logs for each direct report to make sure that there is a sufficient amount of information collected for a complete assessment of the individual's performance. (No performance logs? Start now making informal notes on all aspects of your direct reports' performance over the course of the entire appraisal period.)	☐
April 17	Receive full performance appraisal packet from headquarters. Open packet and make sure that you have one appraiser's manual and at least one appraisal form for each direct report. (Packet missing something? Call Mary Jones at headquarters 404-123-4567.)	☐
April 26	Complete prework for performance appraisal training program.	☐

May 1, 4, or 9	Attend performance appraisal training.	☐
May 12	Complete first performance appraisal for a direct report.	☐
May 17	Complete half of all performance appraisals. Confirm that you have provided information needed by other appraisers.	☐
May 24	Complete all performance appraisals.	☐
May 25	Submit all performance appraisals to reviewer for review and signature. Submit list of individuals and percentage of salary increase recommended to Joe Smith at headquarters. Send to: *joesmith@headquarters.com*	☐
June 1	Receive approved appraisals back from reviewer. Receive salary adjustment approvals back from corporate HR.	☐
June 4	Conduct first performance review. Schedule performance-planning meeting for next fiscal year.	☐
June 15	Complete all performance reviews and scheduling of all performance-planning meetings.	☐
June 22	Submit performance appraisal summary document and HR copies of performance appraisal forms to Joe Smith at headquarters.	☐
July 1	Begin performance-planning discussions for next year.	☐

7.10   We use a lot of self-directed work teams in our organization. Should we evaluate team performance in addition to the performance of individuals? And how do we evaluate the performance of teams?

Team appraisal is difficult. And it may be unfair.

Consider a college example. At the beginning of the semester, the professor divides all of the students into teams, gives each team a research assignment, tells them that they will make a team presentation at the last class meeting, and states that their grade for the course will be based entirely on the quality of the team's work.

One team is made up of Joe, Mary, Dolly, Sharon, and Tim. Four of the five are dedicated, diligent, achievement-oriented, straight-A students. But Dolly is a goof-off. All she wants is the lowest possible passing grade with the minimum possible effort. So throughout the semester she cuts team meetings, ignores assignments, and does nothing on the project. On the last night of class, Joe, Mary, Sharon, and Tim make A-level presentations. Dolly's presentation is an F.

Four As, one F. The professor averages it out and awards the team—and each individual on the team—a B for the course. Joe, Mary, Sharon, and Tim are disgusted. Dolly is tickled pink. The problem with appraising team performance is that it may punish the hardworking and diligent and reward the shiftless and lazy.

Tell Me More

Companies rarely appraise the performance of teams. In the national benchmarking study of best practices in performance appraisal I conducted in 1999, we specifically looked for examples of companies doing performance appraisals on teams. We expected, since so many organizations report that they are using self-directed work teams, that we would find several examples of team appraisal. We found none. There was a great deal of interest in the subject, but no one was doing it.

What companies are doing in assessing the performance of teams is to assess the performance of the individuals on the teams. The team measures matrix, as shown in Figure 7-1, illustrates the difference between measuring performance at the individual level and at the team level.

7.11 We are concerned that people who perform the same may get different ratings from different supervisors. How can we make sure that appraisers apply consistent standards across our organization?

The most effective way to make sure that consistent performance standards are being applied across an organization is to hold cross-calibra-

Figure 7-1. The team measures matrix.

		Competencies/Behaviors	Objectives/Results
Level	**Individual**	Whether or how well the individual cooperates with team members, communicates ideas during team meetings, participates in the team's decision-making processes.	The quality of the written report, turnaround time for the individual's project, accuracy of the advice and information submitted to the team, number and quality of team assignments completed.
	Team	Whether or how well the team runs effective meetings, communicates well as a group, allows all opinions to be heard, comes to consensus on decisions.	The customer satisfaction measures with the team products, the effect of the team's product on increasing quality and reducing cost, the cycle time for the team's entire process.

Competencies/   **Objectives/**
Behaviors   **Results**

Focus

Source: Grote Consulting Corporation.

tion meetings. Appraisers first write their performance appraisals of their subordinates. Before reviewing the appraisals either with their bosses or with the individuals being appraised, they attend a cross-calibration meeting to compare their appraisals and ratings with other managers who supervise similar groups. After the meeting they make any revisions required.

In a typical cross-calibration meeting, a group of managers, all of whom supervise people doing similar jobs at similar levels, meet to go over the appraisals they have written. Each appraiser shares the appraisals she has prepared with the other meeting participants; she also reviews the ones that they have written. They discuss performance expectations and results. By comparing appraisals written by different appraisers, the likelihood of cross-department consistency goes up.

Tell Me More

Cross-calibration meetings are extremely beneficial in ensuring that appraisers from different parts of the organization are applying similar standards and that people performing at similar levels will receive similar performance (and salary increases).

Before the meeting, appraisers finish writing all of their appraisals. They then identify the individuals in their work group whom they consider to be "benchmarks." Benchmarks are those employees whose performance is exactly described by one of the rating labels, whether that performance is superior, or fully successful, or unsatisfactory. They also determine the number of employees they have rated at each level of performance.

During the meeting various appraisers describe the performance of their benchmark employees. Other appraisers ask questions about how the performance rating was determined, what factors other appraisers took into consideration in deciding to rate an individual as needs improvement or superior or fully successful. By developing a common picture of the quality of performance at each level, appraisers are then able to make good judgments about how the performance of each person in their work group should be rated.

Appraisers also talk about performance rating challenges during these meetings. They have the opportunity to ask other raters how they would assess the performance of an individual who succeeded brilliantly in all areas except one, where that one area was a colossal failure. They can compare notes with each other to see if they are being too soft or too tough.

When they reach consensus on what quality of performance is represented by the different performance appraisal ratings, they then can revise the ratings of all of their employees to make sure that they are in line with the ratings for similar levels of performance in other departments of the company.

Another great benefit of conducting cross-calibration (or "rater-reliability") meetings is that it gives appraisers the chance to get confirmation that a particularly poor rating is actually deserved. Then, when the manager is actually delivering the performance appraisal to the poor performer, she will be more confident that the low rating is accurate because it has been reviewed and confirmed by her peers.

7.12   What Is "upward appraisal"?

Upward appraisal is a performance appraisal of a boss written by the subordinates. In organizations that use upward appraisal, after the manager has finished preparing and discussing their performance appraisals with each subordinate, the subordinates individually and anonymously complete a questionnaire about how well the manager manages them. The results are distilled into an anonymous report and given to the manager so that he can learn about his managerial strengths and shortcomings.

Tell Me More

Obviously, one of the best ways to learn how good a job an individual is doing at managing people is to ask the people that he is managing. That's the rationale behind upward appraisal.

In most organizations that use this technique (there aren't too many), as soon as the manager has completed his responsibilities for creating and reviewing the performance appraisals of his staff, each staff member completes a written questionnaire that contains a dozen or so questions about the boss's managerial skills and practices. For example, here are some questions about a manager's practices that might appear on an upward appraisal questionnaire. The respondent would answer each one using a scale from strongly agree to strongly disagree:

My manager:

- Works with me to identify clear and attainable goals.
- Initiates coaching discussions.
- provides honest and constructive feedback about my performance.
- Provides challenging opportunities that maximize the use of my skills.
- Helps me find ways to maintain a healthy balance between work and life.

In addition to questions like these, individuals may also be asked to respond to open-ended questions about the boss's managerial practices and the competencies that the manager either excels in or performs poorly. In another organization, each respondent is asked to identify:

- Two things the manager should do more of
- Two things the manager should keep on doing
- Two things the manager should stop doing.

Each individual's report is sent to the human resources department, which combines the individual responses into a summary report. The information is powerful. The results of upward appraisals not only influence the development decisions a manager makes about enhancing her managerial skills; in some organizations they also directly impact on the manager's compensation.

7.13 Should forced ranking be part of our performance appraisal procedure?

First, a definition. Forced ranking is a recently developed management procedure that requires managers to assign employees into predetermined groups according to their performance, potential, and promotability.

General Electric, the company best known for the procedure, sorts employees into three groups: a top 20 percent on whom rewards, promotions, and stock options are showered; a high-performing middle 70 percent with good futures: and a bottom 10 percent. The bottom 10 percent is unlikely to stay.

GE's not alone. Ranking employees is an everyday practice at highly admired companies such as Microsoft, Cisco Systems, Hewlett-Packard, EDS, PepsiCo, and Sun Microsystems. Sun's performance appraisal system parallels GE's. Hewlett-Packard uses a one to five scale with 15 percent of employees receiving the highest grade and 5 percent receiving a rating of one. PepsiCo ranks workers with a quartiling approach; EDS uses quintiling.

What all these systems have in common is their requirement that managers, in addition to conducting conventional performance appraisals and evaluating how well people have performed against objectives, compare people against each other. Managers must place each person into one of a limited number of categories with a fixed percentage assigned to each one.

Tell Me More

Employee ranking—Jane is better than Bob but not as good as Charlie—has always been a feature of organizational life. What's different now is that companies are formalizing these conversations. They are moving them away from casual exchanges around the water cooler into intense and highly structured meetings that sometimes last two days.

Critics of ranking systems charge that these forced-distribution schemes are subjective, unfair, and discriminatory. Forcing managers to assign a certain fixed percentage into a bottom group seems unfair, particularly when groups are small and are made up of people with unique skills and widely varying assignments. Deliberately culling the bottom of the herd flies in the face of a popular mythology that assumes that everyone is salvageable.

On one point at least, the procedure's critics have it right: Forced ranking systems are certainly discriminatory. They discriminate against the dull and slothful in favor of the bright and energetic. But this discrimination is not only legal, it is mandatory if a company is going to prevail in a tough and competitive market. The arguments that the process is *illegally* discriminatory, however, seem specious: One suit alleges that ranking systems encourage the continuation of a good-old-boy network to the detriment of minorities and females; another puts forth the claim that as a result of companies' concern with encouraging diversity, older white males take a disproportionate hit when the ranking game is played.

A lack of objectivity is another common complaint about ranking systems. But check out what *objective* actually means: "Uninfluenced by emotions or personal prejudices: *an objective critic*. Based on observable phenomena; presented factually: *an objective appraisal*." Ranking systems serve to increase the objectivity of the employee review process by systematizing the complex job of assessing talent. A great benefit of forced ranking systems is that they clarify the criteria the organization uses to assess performance and potential and then force managers to focus on only those criteria in making their judgments.

Employee ranking requires tough decisions in an area where solid, quantitative, numerical data simply don't exist, particularly when one is assessing the individual's potential and promotability. The employee ranking process requires the exercise of honed managerial judgment in a situation where the data are always incomplete and often contradictory—the same managerial judgment that we applaud and reward when it is applied in other areas. But managers make tough decisions based on limited data all the time: which projects to fund, which to shelve, when to react swiftly to a competitor's move, when to let time take its course. Just because the decision isn't based on countable units doesn't mean that the decision isn't objective. Such highly valuable skills as sensitivity to nuance, or the ability to transform adversaries into allies, or the willingness to go the extra mile for a customer, can't be reduced to a quantitative, numerical scheme. Employee ranking is not the same as solving an algebra problem: It can't be reduced to a mathematical algorithm. Hard decisions need to be made in organizations. The data are always imperfect. The forced ranking procedure helps managers make these hard decisions with intelligence and compassion.

Forced ranking's apparent unfairness generates the most protests. The usual scenario presents a hapless manager forced to sit in judgment of his team of uniquely skilled organizational Green Berets, each one doing an excellent job, and to force-rank a portion of them into the company's dunce category. But talent variations do exist, even among real Green Berets. Green Berets may well be the military's best-of-breed, but some demonstrate more courage under fire than others do. Some have better insights about how an attack should be deployed, about which informants are actually double agents. So while everyone in a small department may indeed play a unique role well, some play their roles better than others and offer more potential to play bigger and more challenging roles.

What is never put forth in these fatuous "Green Beret" objections is the equally likely case—the team in question consists of a bunch of organizational Keystone Kops. Now the forced ranking system unfairly compels the manager to place an arbitrary number of dimwits into a superior performance category.

Forced ranking's fairness is most apparent when layoffs become a necessity. When economic necessity mandates reductions in force, is it fair for companies to throw out solid performers and retain marginal ones? And if companies do that, isn't that unfair to their customers? And if companies treat their customers unfairly, isn't the job security of the remaining workers thereby unfairly jeopardized? When layoffs are unavoidable, ranking is the fairest way to proceed.

Employee ranking systems have a worthy goal: to recognize and retain top performers, while improving or removing bottom players. These unpopular systems compel reluctant managers to identify that small minority of staff who make a disproportionate contribution to the organization's success, and to finger those whose departure would likely be beneficial. They guard against spineless managers who are afraid to jettison their laggards.

But too many managers suffer compassion glut. They hate making these tough judgments, preferring to live in a Lake Wobegon world where all the children are above average. A forced ranking procedure compels managers to inform employees honestly about the perceived quality of their work and their long-term potential with the organization. Without the rigor of a forced approach, too many managers continue to push along poor performers with deceptively inflated reviews.

7.14 We are considering either turning our existing performance appraisal form into an Internet-based application or purchasing a web-based performance appraisal system. Is either a good idea?

Yes. There are several significant advantages that a sophisticated, Internet-based performance appraisal system has when compared with a standard paper-and-pencil approach:

- It eliminates the administrative chore of physically delivering forms to appraisers and appraisees.
- It makes it easier for the appraiser to keep track of performance data on a regular basis.
- It can serve as a tickler system to encourage the appraiser to add information and to complete the administrative requirements of the system.
- It can integrate performance appraisal training with the forms and procedural guidelines.
- It can allow a great deal of data-mining, so that the organization can easily get a great deal of information on performance management activities and results throughout the organization.

There are also some major concerns that must be addressed:

- Effective web-based systems that incorporate best practices are expensive.
- Some users may perceive the systems as difficult to learn and cumbersome to use.
- Using a web-based approach may require a significant amount of technical support.
- The ease of meeting the organization's performance management requirements through technology may encourage managers to have fewer face-to-face discussions about performance.
- There are significant security concerns that must be addressed and resolved.

- Web-based systems are most easily used in organizations where almost everyone has easy access to the Internet.

But Internet-based performance management systems certainly represent the future. They make it much easier for managers to meet their performance-management responsibilities and encourage more frequent communication between raters and ratees. One major benchmarking study found that online performance management systems significantly reduce administrative burdens and increase accuracy. Companies that had implemented sophisticated systems also found that automated performance management systems provided these major benefits:

- Increased consistency and reduced subjectivity
- Improved review quality
- Improved timeliness of completion and delivery
- Immediate access for senior managers to performance information throughout their organizations
- Eased entry of new employees into the organization and immediate communication of performance expectations
- Ability to provide just-in-time training at the moment that the user was setting goals or writing an appraisal
- Reduced training costs
- Reduced time spent drafting and reviewing performance appraisals, thus allowing more time for manager/employee interactions
- Allowing for continuous updates of performance expectations

In fact, the results and impact attributed to electronic performance management at some companies are truly staggering. For example, Chrysler Corp., claims that as direct result of automated performance management, 78 percent of managers cited improved quality of feedback, 80 percent cited ease of writing, and 62 percent cited reduced writing time. On the employee side, 83 percent felt review comments were more meaningful, and 78 percent felt that they had received more value-added feedback.

In addition to these benefits to appraisers and appraisees from Internet-based systems, human resources managers and senior executives discover that administrative costs are reduced, reviews are conducted more frequently and with higher quality, and the amount of important information available about performance throughout the organization is far greater and easy to collect than it ever was before.

Chapter 8

Building Performance Excellence

8.1 What does building performance excellence involve?

Building performance excellence requires the manager to do three things. First, the manager is responsible for creating the conditions that motivate. Second, the manager must provide developmental opportunities. Finally, the manager must confront and correct performance problems.

How to create the conditions that motivate was covered thoroughly in Chapter 3 on performance execution. This chapter explores the manager's other two responsibilities: providing developmental opportunities and solving people problems.

8.2 What influences an individual's development?

Most of the factors that influence an individual's ultimate effectiveness have been firmly established by the time the person is a member of an organization. His basic genetic endowment is set; the individual's early family, school, and other experiences (e.g., influential teachers, coaches, pastors, and priests) have long since had their influence.

Since 1982 the Center for Creative Leadership has studied the ways in which successful executives acquire their skills. Their research has identified five broad categories of experiences they found to be developmental, as reported by several hundred managers who analyzed and identified the factors that resulted in their own growth:

- Challenging jobs
- Bosses and other people
- Hardships

- Off-the-job experiences
- Training programs

Tell Me More

1. *Challenging Jobs.* Being given a challenging job is the single most important source of development. Challenging jobs force rapid growth and learning. Dealing with crises, starting up an operation from scratch, fixing up troubled operations—these situations require individuals to cope with pressure and learn quickly. In absolute terms, challenging assignments are the best teacher. They are the most likely to be remembered and teach the greatest variety and largest number of lessons.

2. *Bosses and Other People.* Bosses serve as models. Ask a group of people to think back in their lives to that point when they transitioned from the world of school to the world of work, and then ask how many of them can remember their very first boss. Almost everybody will. Bosses, particularly first bosses, have an enormous impact on our development.

Note that this item is not specifying "good bosses." We can learn as much from bad bosses about how we don't want to act as we can from good bosses who provide admirable models.

3. *Hardships.* Hardships teach us about our limits and allow us to both learn and demonstrate our resilience. Making mistakes, getting stuck in dead-end jobs, surviving serious illness, being denied a well-deserved promotion, enduring life's traumas—all these events cause us to look inward and reflect.

4. *Off-the-Job Experiences.* Experiences off the job, primarily community service, often afford opportunities to acquire and practice leadership skills the job can't offer.

5. *Training Programs.* Training programs, the standard regimen of management development activities, are valuable less for what is learned directly from the training than for the opportunity training presents individuals to build self-confidence by sizing themselves up against peers. The Center for Creative Leadership reports that managers find coursework valuable as a forum for trading tips, picking up different problem-solving methods, and comparing themselves with others.

Red Flag

Coursework and training programs can be used to provide specific skills that an individual is lacking; however, just the fact that a course is available on a topic may suggest that the topic isn't one that will be all that important in bringing about long-term development. Hardly a day passes without a brochure or flyer arriving in the manager's in-basket announcing a new program in presentation skills or finance for the nonfinancial manager or communication skills or some other easily taught, easily learned skill. But genuine development does not come from easily taught and learned skill-development programs.

8.3 How do I determine where I, or someone on my team, should concentrate development efforts?

There are several places to look to come up with good ideas on areas to focus development efforts:

- Personal knowledge
- Achievement orientation and impact and influence competencies
- Performance appraisal feedback
- Information from others
- 360-degree feedback data or employee survey results
- The organization's core competencies
- Personal goals and aspirations

Tell Me More

Personal Knowledge. Development activities can focus on two areas: improving areas of deficiency and enhancing existing strengths. Research on successful development programs consistently comes to the same conclusion: People and organizations benefit more from building on strengths than from shoring up weaknesses. Based on your own knowledge of skills that you or your employees are particularly good or bad at, or information from past performance appraisals, you can identify a strength to be enhanced further or a shortcoming that needs developmental attention.

Achievement Orientation and Impact and Influence Competencies. Several research studies, including those carried out by MIT, the consulting firm Hay/McBer, and Lucent/Bell Labs, confirm that there are two competencies that regularly predict success in organizational life more than any others: "Achievement Orientation" and "Impact and Influence." Development of these two areas should always be considered high priority since they are confirmed predictors of success.

Performance Appraisal Feedback. What did the last performance appraisal say? What were the significant strengths and areas for improvement noted? These are prime sources for development efforts.

Information from Others. Other people with whom you or the individual regularly interact are terrific sources of good data about where development efforts might be well placed. If you have a trusted friend in the organization, ask him what suggestions he might make for your development.

360-Degree Feedback Data or Employee Survey Results. If your organization uses a 360-degree feedback process, the information that it provides will be one of the best sources for suggestions on where development efforts should be placed. If your company conducts employee satisfaction surveys, the results may point out areas where you (and other managers) need to do more work.

The Organization's Core Competencies. If your company has identified competencies that senior management expects everyone to display, these are a primary source of development ideas. Which of the competencies are you most a master of? In which of them do you demonstrate the smallest amount of ability? The competencies you identify are the top targets for development efforts.

Personal Goals and Aspirations. It's your life, it's your career. Where do you want to go with it? What do you want to be when you grow up? What do you need to do to go where you want to be? That's where you should concentrate some development efforts.

8.4   Why is the "achievement orientation" competency so important?

Achievement orientation is almost universally identified as one of the two most important predictors of success in complex, sophisticated organizations. Other terms that are often used for this competency

include results "orientation," "taking initiative," and "entrepreneur-
ship."

How do you know achievement orientation when you see it? Here
are some behavioral indicators.

Achievement Orientation Checklist

☐ *Sets challenging goals for self and others.* "Challenging goals" is a
term consistently tossed around. But what is a "challenging"
goal? It's not just doing the job more cheaply, faster, better.
The operational definition is that a truly challenging goal is one
where the goal-setter recognizes that there's only a fifty-fifty
chance of achieving the target. A challenging goal is a real
stretch—it's not a gimme.

☐ *Takes sustained action in the face of obstacles or adversity.* We all
encounter obstacles. A person with a high drive for results or
achievement orientation will keep getting back up even after
life has knocked her down a couple of times.

☐ *Does more than asked.* Going beyond the call of duty is one of
the leading indicators of a high degree of achievement orientation. The person with a strong results-focus looks for opportunities to do extra work to help others and to make a project
move along more quickly.

☐ *Looks for places where problems might arise and fixes them.* Achievement orientation doesn't mean merely solving problems. It
means actively looking for places where problems might arise
and taking action before the problems occur.

☐ *Actively seeks out interesting projects to work on when the current
assignment is completed.* Even in the midst of a challenging and
demanding assignment, the individual with a high achievement orientation actively scouts out the next assignment.

8.5 Why is the competency of "impact and influence" so important?

"Impact and influence" is the other competency that research regularly
demonstrates as a critical factor in differentiating between the merely
good and the truly great. In studies done of three different job
families—managerial/supervisory, technical/ professional, and sales—
impact and influence was either the highest or second-highest competency that distinguished truly outstanding performers from those

whose performance was fully successful. (Achievement orientation was the other.)

Tell Me More

Other names and labels this competency goes by include networking, strategic influence, persuasive skills, and power motivation. The behavioral indicators of impact and influence are outlined in the following checklist.

Impact and Influence Checklist

- ☐ Builds reliable networks before they are needed.
- ☐ Seeks advice from people who have been successful in promoting similar ideas.
- ☐ Anticipates the effect of an action or proposal on people's image of the speaker.
- ☐ Assembles political coalitions; builds "behind the scenes" support for ideas.
- ☐ Uses group process to lead or influence a group.
- ☐ Anticipates and prepares for others' reactions.

Hot Tip

Do some of the items sound like "playing politics"? That's a common complaint lodged against people who successfully develop and use influence skills. But politics is simply the ability to obtain and use power—a neutral attribute. Remember, the only people who complain about "politics" are the losers.

8.6   How do I create a development plan that works . . . one that actually produces results?

There are eight components to an effective development plan. The best way to construct a workable development plan is simply to take a blank piece of paper and write down your response to each item:

1. Knowledge, skill, or competency area to be developed
2. Benefit to your organization
3. Personal payoff
4. Measures to be used
5. Baseline assessment
6. Resources required
7. Completion date
8. Week-by-week plan

Tell Me More

1. *Knowledge, Skill, or Competency Area to Be Developed.* What is the specific skill that you are going to acquire or enhance? The more specific you can be in your description of the skill you're going to acquire, the easier it will be to determine whether you actually have developed it.

2. *Benefit to Your Organization.* Why is it important to your company that you increase your skill in this area or develop this competency? What difference will it make to the organization? Don't waste development efforts on building skills that don't have a payoff for your company.

3. *Personal Payoff.* What will be the benefit to you if you improve in this area? The clearer you are about the reasons that an improvement in a certain area will provide a specific personal payoff, the less likely you will be to abandon your efforts when the predictable obstacles arise.

4. *Measures to Be Used.* How will you determine whether you actually have made a significant improvement in this area? How will somebody know that you are actually better than you were before? Are there numerical, countable measures? Will comments and reactions from colleagues be sufficient? How will you know that change has occurred? What yardstick will you use to judge your success?

5. *Baseline Assessment.* To start, the individual should take no action other than collect data on how often the developmental area arises in her job and how she handles it when it does arise. Collecting baseline data will achieve several results: It may confirm to the individual that indeed her boss was right when he recommended that this should be an area for concentration. Awareness of the area may immediately generate ideas on how performance could be improved. Collecting baseline data will help demonstrate later that development indeed has occurred. Whatever the developmental need may be, ultimate effectiveness will

be greater if the very first thing the person does is collect his own data to confirm that yes, indeed, this is an area that requires some attention. Answer these questions: How good are you in this area right now? How do you know? What evidence do you have that tells you that this really is an area worth spending time in?

6. *Resources Required.* The resources required are frequently, but never exclusively, financial. If the individual needs to attend a training program or educational experience, the funds will need to be allocated. If the individual needs to purchase a book or computer software to learn skills, somebody will need to write the check. If an offsite visit to another operation is required, somebody will have to spring for the trip. The most important resource required for the execution of most development plans is time. Answer these questions: What will you need in order to complete your plan? Will you need to devote a significant amount of time to your plan's activities? Where will this time come from? Will you need money? How much? Is it in the budget? What management support will you need?

7. *Completion Date.* Thinking in terms of an "annual development plan" is a mistake. A year is far too long. Construct development plans so that something significant can be done in a quarter—that is, within ninety days. If your development goal will take more than three months to complete, it is too big. Break it down into component parts or pick one important area within the overall area to work on. Otherwise, the development plan will fall into the realm of good intentions and be shuffled off into the "one of these days" stack.

8. *Week-by-Week Plan.* A common reason that development plans don't accomplish too much is that we don't break them down into manageable chunks. If you think through what you will need to do to develop a particular skill or competency on a week-by-week basis, you are much more likely to complete the plan since you will have a clear road map of the action you need to take.

8.7 Isn't development the responsibility of the individual? What are the manager's responsibilities for developing subordinates?

The manager has six key responsibilities for the development of subordinates:

1. Identify key individual and organization development needs.
2. Coach the subordinate's selection of areas for developmental concentration.
3. Coach the subordinate's construction of a development plan.
4. Bless the plan/fund the plan.
5. Create developmental opportunities.
6. Follow up to ensure successful execution.

Tell Me More

1. *Identify key individual and organizational development needs.* Although the individual is primarily responsible for his or her own development, the manager needs to be able to recommend areas for consideration. These include both development needs the manager sees in the individual, and opportunities within the manager's work unit where an increase in competence will enhance organizational effectiveness.

2. *Coach the subordinate's selection of areas for developmental concentration.* The manager needs to recommend—sometimes strongly—that developmental attention be paid to some areas first.

3. *Coach the subordinate's construction of a development plan.* The most common mistakes that people make in creating development plans is to make them too big and too general. The manager needs to communicate the value of specificity and the importance of short-term, low goals. Requesting examples or asking questions such as, "How will you actually do that?" and "When do you think you'll have that done?" can be extremely helpful in creating a specific and workable plan.

4. *Bless the plan/fund the plan.* The responsibility for developing a systematic, logical plan is the subordinate's, not the boss's. The manager's appropriate role is first to bless the plan: to review it, ask questions, make suggestions for improvements, and provide counsel and advice. The boss's other responsibility is to fund the plan—to provide whatever resources are needed for the approved plan to be carried out.

5. *Create developmental opportunities.* The best way to create developmental opportunities is to provide the subordinate with challenging work, ongoing feedback on performance, and recognition for task accomplishment.

6. *Follow up to ensure successful execution.* The manager needs to hold individual team members responsible for successful completion of their development plans, just as the manager holds them accountable for successful completion of all other job duties.

8.8   Most development plans seem to involve little more than just signing up for training programs. Where does training fit into a development plan?

Training isn't "development." Training is simply one component in a complete development plan. Here are six suggestions to use training as an effective part of a development process:

1. Never start a development plan with a training program.
2. Identify your objectives first.
3. Contact the trainer.
4. Focus on application.
5. Build alliances.
6. Seek immediate opportunities to practice.

Tell Me More

Training isn't "development." Training is simply one component in a complete development plan.

1. *Never start a development plan with a training program.* Training should never be scheduled as one of the first activities in the plan. At the very beginning of a development process, most people don't know what they need to learn. They have no internally tested data that tell them that the area they have identified is one that they truly need to learn something about and do something different in.

2. *Identify your objectives first.* What is it, as a result of the training program, that the individual will be able to do that he is not now able to do? That is the key question to ask—not what will the person learn or appreciate, but what will he do differently as a result of training? Without some initial data on what the individual is doing right now, it is difficult to formulate worthwhile behavioral change objectives.

3. *Contact the trainer.* If the training is an instructor-led program, call the instructor in advance with a list of personal learning objectives and ask if they will be met. Calling the trainer in advance provides two additional benefits that enhance the learning experience. First, knowing the reasons that this particular individual is attending the program encourages the trainer to make sure that all of those objectives are covered. Second, the facilitator will go out of her way to meet the individual and make sure, over the course of the session, that the program is delivering what was promised.

4. *Focus on application.* Just learning new ideas and techniques and approaches doesn't do any good if they are not applied. Throughout the training program, the primary question each participant should be asking is, How can I apply what I've learned back on the job?

5. *Build alliances.* Training programs provide an additional important benefit independent of whatever subject matter is taught. They allow participants to interact with each other and build their professional network. Look for opportunities to interact with others in the course of the training session.

6. *Seek immediate opportunities to practice.* New skills decay rapidly if they are not immediately put to use.

The need for the manager and the subordinate to conduct a post-program assessment is obvious (but often ignored). The manager who schedules a twenty-minute post-session briefing or requires a one-page bullet-item summary of key points learned (and, more important, actions to be taken based on the program) will not only maximize the dollars spent on training but significantly increase the probability that real development will occur.

Hot Tip

To maximize training's effectiveness, the manager who is concerned with ensuring the development of her subordinates should require the individual to immediately teach the main points, key concepts, and critical techniques to a group of colleagues. Sharing the learning experience maximizes the investment that the organization makes in the individual. More important, anyone who attends a training program with the knowledge that he is going to have to sift the wheat from the chaff and then serve the wheat to a group of colleagues will be a far more active participant in the learning process.

8.9 How can I use the job itself as a developmental experience?

The tasks, assignments, and activities that a person performs on the job can also serve as developmental experiences. In Chapter 3, "Performance Execution," we discussed ways of enriching the developmental nature of a job by deliberately building in challenge and autonomy.

By assigning specific projects to her subordinates, a manager can provide a developmental experience to a subordinate while the person is also meeting his core job responsibilities.

Tell Me More

The Center for Creative Leadership's research indicates that a particular assignment will serve as a developmental opportunity if it has most of these characteristics:

- Ensures that both success and failure are possible and visible.
- Requires aggressive, "take charge" leadership.
- Involves working with new people.
- Requires influencing people, activities, and factors over which the individual has no direct control.
- Involves high task variety.
- Is closely watched by people whose opinions count.

Here are some examples of special assignments that have a high probability of causing real development:

- Planning an offsite meeting or conference
- Going to a college campus as a recruiter
- Running a company meeting or department picnic
- Doing a project with another function
- Managing the visit of a VIP
- Summarizing a new trend, process, or technique and presenting it to others
- Teaching someone how to do something you're skilled at

Too often, we overlook excellent opportunities for development because we simply aren't looking for them. Consider this special assignment and see if it seems to be a genuine development opportunity:

> You will head up a project team made up of people from throughout the organization. Your team will be given a highly measurable and challenging financial goal to achieve, but in the past, every team that has been assigned a similar project has made the goal. You will not have formal authority over anyone on the team but must guide them by means of persuasion and your personal credibility and influence. You will be able to work closely with a large number of people both inside and outside the organization. As project manager, you will interact with

the senior leadership team of both your company and other organizations. You will meet a large number of the community's leaders in the social service, government, and educational domains in both business and social settings. The project and your personal performance will be watched closely by large numbers of influential people. There will be significant rewards for success and penalties for failure. You will work very hard but will be very likely to succeed, since everyone before who has accepted this assignment has succeeded at it. At the end of the project—assuming you also succeed—there will be a major celebration.

Does this not sound like a perfect developmental opportunity? It arises annually in virtually every organization. It's called "United Way Coordinator."

8.10 Should I evaluate the employee's success in completing his development plan as part of the performance appraisal?

No. You may be delighted that the individual has successfully completed a significant development plan, or disappointed that she has ignored all of your suggestions about development. But development isn't performance. Performance appraisal needs to focus exclusively on how well the person did the job that she was paid to do. However, a person's commitment to increasing her capabilities and skills through active involvement in developmental activities will certainly be considered in making other important personnel decisions, such as decisions on promotion, assignment to training programs, assignment of desirable projects, and layoffs.

8.11 I have an employee whose performance is not acceptable. I have had one or two informal conversations with him, but nothing's changed. What should I do?

Most of the time, with most of the people a manager supervises, a word in the ear is sufficient to solve a problem whenever one arises. But when informal, casual conversations aren't successful in bringing about a performance improvement, the manager must plan for and conduct a performance improvement discussion.

Before managers can hold employees responsible for how well they do their job, they must hold themselves responsible for creating the conditions that allow people to do a good job. There are five—and only five—responsibilities that a manager must meet in creating the conditions that allow people to do a good job:

1. Clarify expectations.
2. Provide training.
3. Arrange appropriate consequences.
4. Provide feedback.
5. Remove obstacles.

Tell Me More

The following checklist covers each one of the manager's responsibilities and provides two questions to ask to make sure that you have met your responsibilities.

1. *Clarify expectations.* The manager is responsible for clearly specifying the gap between the desired performance and the actual performance.

☐ Is the individual able to explain exactly what is expected?
☐ Does the individual understand the exact gap between desired performance and actual performance?

2. *Provide training.* The manager is responsible for making sure that the employee has been given the training necessary to do the job.

☐ Does the individual have the knowledge and skills needed to do the job?
☐ Has the individual received the same training as other individuals?

3. *Arrange appropriate consequences.* The manager is responsible for making sure that good job performance generates positive consequences and that poor job performance leads to adverse consequences.

☐ What happens to the individual: 1) when he performs properly; 2) when he performs poorly?

☐ Does doing the job properly or quickly produce unpleasant consequences?

4. *Provide feedback.* The manager is responsible for making sure that the employee knows exactly how well or how poorly he is doing.

☐ How does the individual know exactly what's expected of her?
☐ How does the individual know exactly how well or how poorly he's doing?

5. *Remove obstacles.* The manager is responsible for making sure that nothing interferes with good job performance.

☐ What would prevent the individual from doing the job right if he wanted to?
☐ Does the individual have the time, the tools, the equipment, the authority, and the support needed to do the job?

Once the manager has met these five responsibilities, she has done all that she is responsible for. The responsibility for good job performance now shifts to the employee.

Hot Tip

Don't ever say "We have a problem . . ." when talking to an employee about a performance problem. "We" never have a problem. Either you as the manager have a problem because you haven't met your responsibilities for creating the conditions that allow the employee to perform properly, or the employee has a problem because he isn't performing properly in spite of the fact that the manager has made it possible for him to do so.

8.12 How do I identify exactly what the gap is between the desired performance and the employee's actual performance?

Identifying the gap between desired and actual performance is the most difficult part of solving performance problems. The reason is that we usually define the problem in very general and abstract terms (e.g., "Harriet's got an attitude problem"), or we label the individual with an accusation (e.g., "George is a slacker" or "Tony isn't a team player"), or we use metaphors (e.g., "Sally isn't keeping her nose to the grindstone or her shoulder to the wheel"). Although these statements may be true, none of them is helpful in determining what the exact difference is between what we want the individual to do and what the person is actually doing.

If the manager doesn't clearly define the gap between what he wants and what he gets, he is not going to be successful in bringing about a change in the employee's performance. The first step, therefore, is to define clearly and specifically what exactly the employee is doing that causes us concern, and then identify exactly what it is that we want the individual to do. The easiest way to do this is to imagine that you are talking with the individual about the situation. Quite sincerely, the employee says, "Boss, in this area that we're talking about, I just don't understand exactly what it is that you want me to do. I'll do anything you want, but please tell me exactly what it is that I need to do for you to feel like I'm meeting your expectations?"

How would you respond to that question—what would you say? Whatever you would say, write your answer down. It will probably be a very clear and unemotional statement of exactly what the desired performance is, without any generalizations or abstractions or labels.

Then assume that the employee asks, "Boss, I know I'm letting you down, but I don't know exactly what it is that I'm doing wrong. Would you please tell me exactly what it is that I am doing that causes you concern?"

Again, what would you say? And again, write down whatever you would say because it will probably be a very clear statement of the actual performance.

Tell Me More

Here are some examples of clear statements of desired and actual performance.

Example 1

Issue: Smoking in an inappropriate area.
Desired: Only smoke in the company's official smoking areas.
Actual: Bill Monroe was smoking outside the main entrance

to the building. Although he was outside the building, he was not in one of the official smoking areas.

Example 2

Issue: Doing personal business on company time.

Desired: Do only company business when you are at work. Let me know when an assigned project has been completed, or ask one of your other team members if you can help them.

Actual: Earlier this morning I noticed you reading a magazine ten minutes before your lunch period began.

Example 3

Issue: Poor attendance.

Desired: Be here, at your desk, fully prepared and ready to work every day at 8:30 A.M.

Actual: On January 23, Susan arrived at her desk at 8:47 A.M. On February 1, she got to her desk just before 9:00 A.M. This morning she arrived at her desk at 8:37 A.M.

Many times, when you are dealing with an issue that concerns the quality of the individual's performance, it's difficult to come up with specific and precise statements of the gap between desired and actual performance. In this case, include examples of the difference between what you want and what you get:

Example 4

Issue: Lack of teamwork.

Desired: Every person in the department should demonstrate teamwork.

Actual: Tony doesn't always act as a team player. For example, when Charles and Olivia asked him for help with their project, Tony said, "That's not in my job description." When I asked everyone to submit one or two suggestions on how we could operate more effectively as a team, Tony was the only person in the department who did not submit any suggestions.

Red Flag

Until you can specify what the gap is between desired and actual performance on the employee's part, you haven't earned the right to ask the employee to close the gap.

8.13 How do I make sure that I'm on solid ground before beginning the discussion about poor performance?

The most important step is to clearly identify the difference between the desired performance and the employee's actual performance. Several other pieces of preparation help ensure that you are successful in your meeting with the individual:

1. Identify the impact.
2. Determine the consequences.
3. Check for defensibility.

Tell Me More

1. *Identify the impact.* What are the good business reasons that demand that the problem be solved? What difference does it make if the employee comes to work a few minutes late, or smokes outside the building but not in an official smoking area, or doesn't act as a team player? So what if Margie spends a few minutes reading a magazine?

In the course of a discussion about a need for performance improvement, it's common for the employee to respond to the manager's request for change by arguing that what he is doing is no big deal and that the manager is making mountains out of molehills. The manager's usual response to these objections is to fall back on a power and authority position: I am the boss; it is a rule. But power and authority don't help much in bringing about a genuine agreement to change. A better approach is to think through the impact—the good business reasons why the organization or the manager has the performance expectation under discussion. If the manager has written down a list of all the reasons why the rule or expectation is important, it will be easy for her to say, "Yes, Margie, I know that it does sound like a minor item. But actually, it's quite important. Let me go over the good business reasons why we have this expectation of our staff."

2. *Determine the consequences*. In spite of knowing that what he's doing creates a problem for the organization, and in spite of knowing why it's a problem, the employee may still decide to continue to smoke in inappropriate locations, or do personal business on company time, or not act as a team player. What are the logical consequences of that decision?

The one that immediately springs to most managers' minds is: further disciplinary action, up to and including discharge. And although that may be true, the threat of disciplinary action and discharge is not usually the most effective action available to the manager. There are often far more powerful adverse consequences available to the manager when employees decide not to do what they're being paid to do. For example, the manager could:

- Restrict smoking breaks altogether.
- Impose closer supervision.
- Refuse to allow participation on the annual event planning committee.
- Deny a request to attend an out-of-town conference.

It may well be that these consequences have far more power in convincing someone to straighten up and solve a problem than if the manager merely tells the employee, "I'm going to write you up."

Hot Tip

Is reviewing the logical consequences of failing to solve the problem the same as threatening to punish the employee if she doesn't change behavior? Not quite. All of the choices people make in life, including their on-the-job choices, have consequences. All the manager is doing is advising the individual of what the natural consequences will be if the individual decides not to do what she is getting paid to do. Some of the logical consequences of continued poor performance have nothing to do with a manager's inflicting punishment. For example, loss of coworkers' respect is a natural consequence of goofing off. But there's no thought of punishment here.

---

3. *Check for defensibility.* Any disciplinary action or discharge can be challenged. To make sure that the action you're planning to take will survive a legal challenge, ask and answer these five questions:

1. Did the employee clearly understand the rule or policy that was violated?
2. Did the employee know in advance that such conduct would be subject to disciplinary action?
3. Was the rule violated reasonably related to the safe, efficient, and orderly operation of the business?
4. Is there substantial evidence that the employee actually did violate the rule?
5. Is the action planned reasonably related to the seriousness of the offense, the employee's record with the organization, and action taken with other employees who have committed a similar offense?

If the answer to any of the questions is "No" or "I'm not sure," you're not ready for a formal disciplinary transaction.

8.14   How do I get the discussion off to a good start?

Probably the toughest ten seconds in management comes when the manager has told the employee that they need to get together to talk about a problem. The appointed time comes, the employee arrives in the manager's doorway, knocks, and says, "You wanted to see me, boss?" What should the manager say to start off the meeting?

Here's a script that will work well:

Say, " [*Employee's name*], I have a problem."
State the actual and desired performance.
Say, "Tell me about it," or some similar statement.

Tell Me More

In an actual situation, the script might go like this: "Margie, I have a problem that I need to talk over with you. It's important that you spend all of your work time actually doing your work, but recently I've noticed that you seem to spend quite a bit of time on personal affairs. For example, last week I noticed that you were working on your income tax return, and then this morning, about ten minutes before lunch, I noticed that you were reading a magazine. Help me understand what's going on."

In starting the conversation by saying, "Margie, I have a problem. . . ," the manager has done three things right. First, she has used the person's name. Second, she has gotten right to the point and not wasted time on irrelevant small talk. Finally, she has taken personal responsibility—I have a problem.

Hot Tip

At the end of this meeting, Margie may well have a problem. But at the beginning of the meeting, it's good to avoid using the accusatory "You have a problem" or the inaccurate "We have a problem."

The manager then proceeded to state the specific concern—the actual and desired performance. The manager didn't accuse Margie of anything, or use generalizations or abstractions. She simply stated very straightforwardly the specific difference between the desired performance and Margie's actual performance.

Finally, the manager placed the conversational ball in the employee's court when she said, "Help me understand what's going on." By doing this, you avoid the most common error managers make when they begin a performance improvement discussion—talking too much. By asking the employee to respond, the manager can listen to what the individual has to say about the situation.

Hot Tip

When you listen to the employee, what should you be listening for? You want to determine whether there is any new information that, if it's confirmed, would cause you not to proceed with whatever action you were intending to take when the meeting started. For example, the manager is about to take a formal disciplinary step with George for repeatedly coming to work late. In answer to the manager's opening request to "tell me about it," George reveals that his teenage daughter is on drugs and when he's been late, it's because he's been getting his daughter out of jail. Assuming it's true, the manager can immediately shift gears and start explaining the company's employee assistance program to George.

Red Flag

Never begin a discussion with an employee about a problem by announcing your intention to take a formal step of disciplinary action. Instead, start by explaining your concern, then listen to what the individual has to say. Only when you've heard the employee's response and confirmed that there is no reason not to proceed with the disciplinary action you intended to take should you advise the employee that the discussion will be a formal disciplinary transaction.

8.15   How do I get someone to agree to change and correct a problem?

Begin by writing down a clear and unarguable statement of the difference between desired performance and actual performance. If you can't write down exactly what you want and exactly what the employee is doing that concerns you, there is no way that you can get the individual to agree to change.

Next, simply ask for the agreement to change. Say, "Margie, I need for you to agree that in the future you will spend all of your work time doing your assigned projects and that you'll let me know when you've finished so that you can immediately get to work on the next project. May I have your agreement?"

It's difficult for a person not to agree, since all you are asking for is that the individual agree to do what she is being paid to do.

Tell Me More

From time to time you may get a response that the expected performance really isn't all that important or that the manager is being unreasonable. That's why, as part of your preparation, it's good to write down a list of the good business reasons that the problem must be solved. If Margie responds, "Oh, it's no big deal. Everybody does personal stuff from time to time. You're making a mountain out of a molehill," the well-prepared manager can comfortably respond, "Actually, Margie, that's not true. It is important . . . let me tell you why. When others see you doing personal business, they feel that they can do the same thing, or they may resent you for making them work harder since you're working less. If customers come by and see you reading a magazine, they'll wonder about what kind of employees we hire here. Every minute that you spend on your personal affairs is a minute that is not being spent on company business, so we're paying for something that we're not getting. That's why it's important for you to agree that you'll always work on your assigned projects and save personal affairs for your breaks and lunch period. May I have your agreement?"

Hot Tip

Notice that the manager never made reference to "I'm the boss; it's a rule" when she responded to Margie. Of course, the manager is the boss; of course it is a rule. But the power-and-authority approach won't be nearly as effective in getting Margie to agree to change as explaining the good business reasons the company has the rule and requesting her agreement.

8.16 How do I document a performance improvement discussion?

When a manager documents a performance improvement discussion or a formal disciplinary transaction, what is it that the manager is actually documenting?

Too many managers think that what they are documenting is the existence of a problem. That's a mistake. You are not documenting the existence of a problem. You are documenting the *discussion* that you and the employee had about the problem.

The best way to document a performance discussion is to send the employee a memo summarizing your conversation and the employee's agreement to correct the problem as soon as you have completed the discussions.

Tell Me More

The following information should be in the memo about your performance discussion:

- The names of the supervisor, the employee, and any witnesses who were present.
- The date on which the discussion took place (and the location, if significant).
- The specific problem that caused the transaction to occur.
- A record of all previous conversations about the problem and the dates on which each of those conversations occurred. This record should include formal disciplinary conversations, coaching sessions, and casual conversations (even though no record of the conversation may have been made).
- A description of the continuing problems that have been experienced since the earlier conversations took place.
- A statement that the situation must be corrected (not "improved") and the specific change that must be made.
- A statement of the fact that failure to correct the problem may lead to more serious disciplinary action.
- A statement that in addition to solving the immediate problem, the organization expects the employee to maintain an acceptable level of performance in every area of his job.
- A record of the agreement made by the employee to correct the problem.
- A record of any action the employee agreed to take in order to bring about the correction.
- A closing statement that expresses the supervisor's belief that the problem will in fact be corrected and that the employee will perform properly in the future.

Hot Tip

After the supervisor has written the memo, the best way to handle the delivery to the employee is to actually sit down with the individual and review it with him. This confirms the importance that the supervisor places on correcting the problem and allows the supervisor to again gain the employee's agreement that the problem will in fact be solved.

8.17 The individual's quality and quantity of work are okay. It's his attitude that's the problem. How do I solve an attitude problem?

Ask any group of managers what the most common "people problem" they encounter is and they will uniformly answer, "Attitude problems."

One of the reasons that attitude problems seem so hard to resolve is that almost anything qualifies as an attitude problem. Is the employee a loner, unwilling to participate in team activities? He's got an attitude problem. Is she egotistical, grabbing all of the credit for others' work? She's got an attitude problem. Does he pick his nose and make rude noises? Ah, another attitude problem.

This step-by-step checklist will help you to confront and resolve attitude problems.

Checklist for Resolving Attitude Problems

- ☐ Narrow the issue to the specific problem or concern.
- ☐ Write down the specific verbal and physical behaviors and actions that concern you.
- ☐ Track the frequency.
- ☐ Identify the impact.
- ☐ Discuss the situation with the individual.
- ☐ Determine whether the individual has a logical reason for the behavior.
- ☐ Tell the individual to stop engaging in the problem behavior.
- ☐ Tell the individual what behavior is required: courteous, cooperative, and helpful.

Tell Me More

▪ *Narrow the issue to the specific problem or concern.* Begin by identifying the specific type of behavior that you are concerned with. Here is a list of various behaviors that could be labeled as attitude problems.

Identify the one that comes the closest to the actual behavior of the individual whose performance you're concerned with:

Annoying /offensive behavior   Insensitive to others
Careless/frivolous   Insubordinate
Complaining   Lazy
Defensive   Negative/cynical
Disruptive   Pouting
Egotistical /credit-grabbing   Rude/surly /inconsiderate
Explosive   Quarrelsome
Inattentive to work   Socializing

- *Write down the specific verbal and physical behaviors and actions that concern you.* The requirement that you write down the items that concern you will force you to focus on specifics. And don't forget to record the nonverbal behaviors (i.e., rolling of the eyes, clenching fists, staring off into space). Pretend you're a movie camera or a tape recorder actually recording exactly what it is that's unfolding in front of you.

- *Track the frequency.* Make a record of how often the various behaviors that concern you arise.

- *Identify the impact.* Make a list of the good business reasons that this behavior must stop.

- *Discuss the situation with the individual.* Explain that the behavior is causing a problem.

- *Determine whether the individual has a logical reason for the behavior.* It is possible that the person may be unaware of what he's doing or doesn't realize that it's distracting to others. It may also turn out that the "attitude problem" you've identified is a symptom of a more serious problem that needs a referral to the employee assistance program.

- *Tell the individual to stop engaging in the problem behavior.* Too often, supervisors fail to take this key step. You must directly tell the person to stop doing whatever it is that he is doing.

- *Tell the individual what behavior is required: courteous, cooperative, and helpful.* Unfortunately, many managers feel that they have to live with what the person is and thereby accept a lot of inappropriate behaviors. This is not true. Supervisors put up with way too much crap. Every organization has the right to demand that everyone who is on the payroll act in a courteous, cooperative, and helpful manner. If the employee says, "Well, that's not in my job description," grab his job description and write it in. If he says, "Well, that's just the way I am," tell him that he will need to find a job with another employer that is willing to accept him just the way he is, because you are not.

8.18 The individual's performance is very good, but her attendance record is spotty. How do I convince someone that we need to come to work, on time, every day?

Start by making your attendance expectation clear. The attendance expectation the organization has of every single employee is the same everywhere: "We expect each employee to come to work every day, on time, fully prepared, clean, straight, and sober, for the full duration of the scheduled workday." Any variance from that is a variance from the company's expectations.

Red Flag

The most important issue to concentrate on in dealing with attendance problems is the effect of the absence, not its cause. Supervisors must continually point out to people with spotty attendance records that ultimately the cause of any absence is irrelevant—only the effect counts. The point is a simple one: Regardless of the quality and truthfulness of the excuse, if the employee doesn't come to work, the employee's job doesn't get done. We can't justify Bobbie Sue's nonperformance to customers simply because she had a really good excuse for not showing up.

Tell Me More

Many people erroneously believe that if they have some sick leave available, then it's okay to take off some time. This is not true. Sick leave has no relationship to vacations or holidays or other forms of time off. Sick leave is an *insurance policy*, just like life insurance or collision coverage on your car. Just because we give you life insurance doesn't mean we want you to die; just because you have collision insurance doesn't mean you want to have a car accident. The purpose of sick leave is to provide salary continuation for a certain number of days when the employee is unable to work for a specifically defined set of reasons. But it has nothing to do with the organization's attendance expectation.

Hot Tip

Some supervisors erroneously believe that if the reason for absence is accurate, and the person is not a liar or a malingerer, the company must tolerate and accommodate the employee. This is not correct and is unfair to the employee's coworkers, who must take up the slack when the absentee is missing. The statement that the supervisor needs to make to the employee is, "Sally, I understand that you may have child-care problems/medical difficulties/car troubles/runaway pets. The fact is, I need someone who can show up for work every day. If you can't come to work every day that you're scheduled, I will need to find someone who can. Now what are you going to do so that you can meet your responsibility for showing up on time every day?"

People often don't realize that courts and arbitrators have consistently upheld the right of an organization to terminate employees for failure to maintain regular attendance even when all of their absences have been for legitimate medical necessity, each has been confirmed by medical certification, and the employee has "sick leave" in the bank.

In writing the statements of desired and actual performance in preparation for the discussion with the employee, avoid writing down the excuses the employee has offered. The statement of desired performance should always read: "Be at work, on time, every day." The statement of the individual's actual performance should read: "On [*dates*] Betty Jo was absent and on [*dates*] Betty Jo was late." Then concentrate on writing a complete summary of the impact of the problem—all the things that don't get done or go wrong because the employee wasn't there.

Hot Tip

An effective way to get control of attendance and reduce absenteeism is to compute the company's or a specific department's average absence rate. Then concentrate on those people whose attendance record is below average. The advantage of this approach is that it avoids considerations of the cause of the absences. You can then say to the employee, "The average absence rate in your department was 4.6 percent, Joe, but your personal absence rate was 5.5 percent." Even better, it gives the employee a reasonable target to shoot for; for example, "We realize you can't be perfect, Joe. All we want you to do is be just a little better than average." As the people with attendance problems improve to better than average, the overall average absence rate goes down.

If an employee ever challenges a supervisor who's discussing attendance by whining, "Well, you don't want me to come to work when I'm sick, do you?" the appropriate answer is, "Yes, we do. We want every employee to be at work every day." This is a hard-line response, but is sometimes necessary with hard-line cases.

Hot Tip

In dealing with attendance problems, never ask the employee to improve. Ask the employee to correct the problem. You don't want improvement, you want a total and complete correction.

Red Flag

When taking disciplinary action or terminating an employee because of an attendance problem, never use the phrase, "Excessive absences." That suggests that there is some standard that the employee has exceeded. Instead, say, "Failure to maintain regular attendance." What is regular attendance? Coming to work, on time, every day.

8.19 Our discipline system seems harsh and inappropriate for professional employees with its warnings and reprimands and suspensions without pay. Is there a better approach?

The traditional "progressive discipline system," with its criminal-justice mentality and its use of punitive warnings and reprimands and probation and suspensions without pay, is outmoded. Discipline Without Punishment is a more effective approach that should be adopted by every organization.

Tell Me More

Like conventional approaches, the Discipline Without Punishment performance management system provides a progressive series of steps to handle everyday problems of absenteeism, bad attitudes, and poor performance. Discipline Without Punishment rejects traditional punitive disciplinary responses, however. Reprimands, warnings, demotions, and unpaid disciplinary suspensions are eliminated. Instead of punishing employees for their misdeeds, the system requires employees to take personal responsibility for their own behavior and to make real decisions about their own careers.

When informal coaching conversations and performance improvement discussions are unsuccessful in solving a performance or behavior problem, the first level of formal disciplinary action is a Reminder 1. The supervisor discusses the problem and reminds the employee of his responsibility to meet the organization's standards. The transaction is formally documented on a worksheet that the supervisor retains.

If the problem continues, the supervisor holds a Reminder 2 discussion. The supervisor again talks to the employee and gains her agreement to solve the problem. After the meeting, the supervisor documents their discussion and the employee's commitment to solve the problem, this time in a written memo to the employee.

Although the use of the term *Reminder* seems gentle, it is actually tougher and more appropriate. Instead of warning the individual what we're going to do the next time we catch him misbehaving, or reprimanding him as we would a six-year-old, we remind him of two things: first, the rule or expectation that the company has, which he has violated; second, the fact that it is his responsibility to do the job that he's being paid to do.

The final step of Discipline Without Punishment is the "decision-making leave." The employee is suspended for a day and told to return the day after the leave with a final decision: either to solve the immediate problem and make a "total performance commitment" to fully acceptable performance in every area of the job, or to resign and seek more satisfying employment elsewhere. The employee is paid for the day he is on decision-making leave to demonstrate the company's good-faith desire to see him change and stay. He is also formally notified that if another problem requiring disciplinary action arises, he will be terminated. If another problem does arise, discharge follows.

Changing the names of the initial steps from oral warnings and written reprimands to Reminder 1 and Reminder 2 eliminates the inappropriate focus on the method of documentation. Paying the employee for the day of suspension changes the supervisor's role from adversary to coach, eliminates money as an issue, reduces the possibility of hostile behavior or workplace violence, encourages supervisors to act rapidly and not wait until a nuisance has become a crisis, and—perhaps most important—makes you look good to a jury.

8.20 Why should we suspend the employee as a final step of our discipline system? Why not just issue a final written warning, or create a performance improvement plan, or place the individual on probation?

At the final step of a discipline procedure, when earlier formal discussions have failed to convince the employee to change behavior and return to fully acceptable performance, a dramatic gesture is required to clearly communicate that the end is at hand. No other final step has as much power as a formal suspension from work as a final disciplinary step because it:

- Allows a "cooling off" period.
- Communicates the seriousness of the issue.
- Demonstrates management's resolve to get the problem solved.
- Provides the employee with time to think.
- Previews unemployment.
- Is accepted by third parties as "sufficient notice."

Tell Me More

The last item may be the most important. Today, almost any termination can be challenged. Typically, the first question that the arbitrator or unemployment hearing officer or other third party will ask is, "Was the employee aware of the seriousness of the situation? Did he fully understand that his job was at risk?" Arbitrators and others have universally accepted a suspension as "sufficient notice" that the individual's job is in jeopardy.

8.21 If a suspension is the best final step strategy, why should we pay the employee for the time he is away on suspension?

There are several reasons that it makes sense to pay the employee for the day he is away from work on decision-making leave. As a practice, the paid suspension:

- Changes the supervisor's role from adversary to coach.
- Demonstrates the company's good faith.
- Is more consistent with organizational values.
- Eliminates money as an issue.
- Doesn't harm the employee's family.
- Reduces anger, hostility, and the risk of workplace violence.
- Makes you look good to a jury.

Tell Me More

Again, the last reason may be the most important. If a discharged employee challenges his termination, then regardless of the facts and regardless of the law, the underlying issue will always be, Was the company fair? When the organization can demonstrate that not only did it have a series of well-documented, progressively more serious discussions with the employee, but it also gave the individual a day at its own expense to think about whether he could perform at a minimally acceptable level and the individual didn't live up to his own commitment, no stronger argument to support termination can be made.

8.22 Will Discipline Without Punishment work in my organization?

Yes. Discipline Without Punishment solves performance problems promptly and permanently by placing the responsibility for change exactly where it belongs—with the individual. The core concept of giving an individual whose performance is not acceptable a day at the company's expense to make a final decision about whether he can meet the organization's expectations and is willing to make an affirmative commitment to excellence in every area of the job is appropriate at any level in the organization.

Tell Me More

The Discipline Without Punishment approach significantly reduces exposure to lawsuits and equal employment opportunity (EEO) complaints resulting from unfair or inconsistent disciplinary action. Once employees set their own standards and agree to them, it's a lot harder for them to say they didn't understand the rules. If a termination is ever challenged, the decision-making leave will demonstrate that your organization took every action possible to rehabilitate the individual.

Service and professional organizations frequently reject traditional progressive-discipline approaches as too "blue collar" for their sophisticated, better-educated workforce. As a result, they often end up with no system at all and handle everything on an inconsistent, ad hoc basis. Discipline Without Punishment is particularly appropriate for today's knowledge workers.

Traditional discipline approaches may indeed convince some problem employees to shape up, others to ship out. But punitive tactics will not produce employees who are genuinely committed to the goals of the enterprise and the policies and rules by which it operates. We can punish people into compliance. We cannot punish people into commitment.

The greatest flaw with the conventional progressive-discipline approach is simply that it asks too little. The traditional system takes a problem employee, punishes him, and leaves the organization with nothing more than a punished problem employee. The Discipline Without Punishment system requires the problem employee to become one of two things: either a good employee or an ex-employee.

Chapter 9

One Final Question

9.1 Now that all is said and done, is performance appraisal really all that important?

Yes. Used well, performance appraisal can be the most powerful tool an organization has to ensure the achievement of strategic goals, to focus the energy of organization members on the achievement of its mission, and to reinforce the importance of everyone's living up to the company's vision and values.

In too many organizations, the performance appraisal system is seen only as a personnel department devise for telling Charlie how he's doing and for justifying Sally's 3 percent raise. Those functions are important, but they are secondary. What is genuinely important is making sure that all employees in the organization understand that there is a direct connection between their performance and the achievement of the company's mission.

Not long ago, I delivered the closing general session address at a large conference of human resources executives. The topic was "Performance Management: Best Practices, New Directions." There must have been 600 VPs of human resources from Fortune 1000 companies in the audience.

When I was making my point about the need for tight integration between a company's performance appraisal procedures and its overall strategic goals, I said to the audience: "Let me ask you three questions. For each question, raise your hand if the answer is true, and look around the room so that you collect the same data that I am collecting. First question—does your company have a formal performance appraisal system? If you do, raise your hand."

Of the 600 people in the audience, about 587 hands went up.

"Second question," I said. "Does your company have a formal, written-down-on-paper mission statement or statement of vision and values? If you do, raise your hand."

Of the 600 people in the audience, about 592 hands went up.

"Last question," I said. "How many of you can take your performance appraisal form in your left hand and your mission statement in your right hand, and walk up to one of your employees and say, 'Harry, look! Do you see where the words in the performance appraisal and the words in the mission statement are the *same words*?' If you can, raise your hand."

Maybe nineteen hands went up.

The point is obvious. If employees don't see any connection between what the organization says is important in its mission statement or its pronouncement of vision and values and what the employees are held accountable for in their performance appraisal, they will become cynical about the importance of the stated mission. Too often, senior organizational leaders expend enormous intellectual and emotional energy developing a statement of the organization's mission or values that fully captures and accurately expresses what these top dogs consider to be truly important. But if all that happens is that these noble words are transformed onto a brass plaque that sits on the wall behind the receptionist's left shoulder, then people will see the mission statement as merely a corporate exercise with no impact on day-to-day business.

If, however, the performance appraisal form incorporates the mission statement—and if employees are assessed on how well they demonstrate the organization's values, and if assessors must rate how well each person did in helping the organization achieve its strategic plan—then people will quickly realize that the mission statement is more than just the end-product of a passing fad. Only when they are held accountable for acting in ways that support the mission and the values will they take seriously the words on the plaque. This is the basis of strategy-based performance management, and it is illustrated in Figure 9-1.

More than any other tool in the organizational arsenal, the performance appraisal process has the power to direct the attention and energy of every organization member toward the achievement of strategic goals and corporate values. That's why the genuinely important items—mission, organizational objectives, vision and values, core competencies—are at the top of Figure 9-1.

Although performance appraisal serves many important functional duties, performance appraisal is not an end in itself. Performance appraisal, used to its maximum benefit, is the means by which everyone in the organization understands and is held accountable for meeting truly important objectives.

Figure 9-1. Strategy-based performance management.

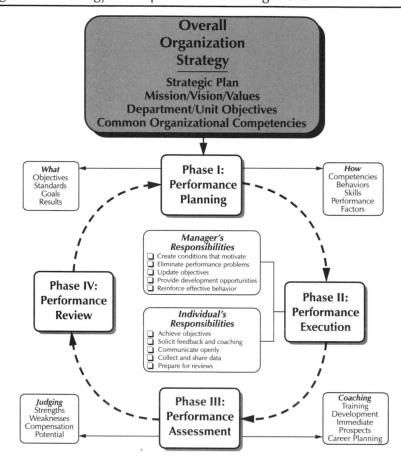

Source: Grote Consulting Corporation.

Index

229

About the Author

Dick Grote is one of America's most successful and best-known authors, consultants, and speakers. He specializes in leadership, performance management, and building organizational excellence.

Trained as an industrial engineer, he joined General Electric after college and graduated from GE's acclaimed Manufacturing Management Training Program. Dick spent a total of fifteen years with General Electric, United Airlines, and PepsiCo, the last five as Frito-Lay's corporate director of training and development. There he invented the innovative "Discipline Without Punishment" performance management system, the unique approach that solves people problems with dignity and grace.

On August 1, 1977, he left Frito-Lay to become a corporate consultant. He created Performance Systems Corporation and built it into a multimillion-dollar firm employing over a dozen consultants. Ten years to the day that he started Performance Systems—July 31, 1987—he sold the firm. For the next two and a half years he traveled extensively, lived on a houseboat in Kashmir, earned a master's degree in renaissance art from Southern Methodist University, and took groups of young junior high and high school musicians on concert tours of Moscow, St. Petersburg, Riga, Latvia, and Prague.

On January 1, 1990, he returned to consulting, creating Grote Consulting Corporation. His clients include some of the largest and most prestigious organizations, public and private, in North America, Western Europe, and Southeast Asia.

Dick's articles and essays have appeared in the *Harvard Business Review*, *The Wall Street Journal*, *Across the Board*, and over two dozen other business and human resources magazines and journals. He is adjunct professor of management at the University of Dallas Graduate School. For five years he was a commentator on life in the workplace for National Public Radio. A platform master, Dick Grote speaks regularly at large human resources and general management conferences. His most recent books, *Discipline Without Punishment* and *The Complete Guide to Performance Appraisal*, were published by the American Management Association. They were both major book club selections and have recently been published in Chinese and Arabic. His video series, *Respect and Responsibility*, was produced by Paramount Pictures.

Dick Grote has been interviewed about his work by *Fortune, Psychology Today, The Wall Street Journal, Harvard Business Review*, and *Business Week*. In 1999 he served as a subject matter expert for the national benchmarking study of best practices in performance management sponsored by the American Productivity & Quality Center, Linkage Inc., and DDI. General Kenneth Minihan, director of the National Security Agency, awarded Dick a medal for his work in creating NSA's performance management system. (He sent the medal home to Mom.) In college he was a member of Colgate University's retired undefeated GE College Quiz Bowl Team. At the age of fifty-nine, he still competes regularly in 5K and 10K races (occasionally bringing home a third-place trophy). Dick Grote's biography has been included in *Who's Who in America* every year since 1979.

In 2002, *Workforce* magazine published a list of the eighty people, events, and trends that shaped HR in the past century. Dick Grote's work in the evolution of performance appraisal came in at number nineteen (ahead of war, but well behind Peter Drucker and Betty Friedan and the PC).